0134 13451550

PATERSON LIBRARY COMMONS
CONFEDERATION COLLEGE

0000
33.00

Educational Policy Studies

A Practical Approach

Jerome G. Delaney

MAR - 8 2011

Detselig Enterprises Ltd.

Calgary, Alberta, Canada

SINCE THIS ITEM
IS NO LONGER IN DEMAND
PATERSON LIBRARY COMMONS
IS OFFERING IT FOR SALE

Educational Policy Studies

© 2002 Jerome Delaney

National Library of Canada Cataloguing in Publication Data

Delaney, Jerome G.

Educational policy studies

Includes bibliographical references and index.

ISBN 978-1-55059-218-4

1. Education and state. I. Title.

LC71.D44   2002   379   C2002-910008-9

Detselig Enterprises Ltd.
210-1220 Kensington Rd. N.W., Calgary, AB T2N 3P5
Phone: (403) 283-0900/Fax: (403) 283-6947
E-mail: temeron@telusplanet.net
www.temerondetselig.com

All rights reserved. No part of this book may be reproduced in any form or by any means without permission in writing from the publisher.

We acknowledge the financial support of the Government of Canada through the Book Publishing Industry Development Program (BPIDP) for our publishing activities.

ISBN 978-1-55059-218-4

SAN 115-0324

Printed in Canada

SINCE THIS ITEM
IS NO LONGER IN DEMAND
PATERSON LIBRARY COMMON-
IS OFFERING IT FOR SALE

DEDICATION
To my wife, Philomena

CONTENTS

PREFACE

Educational Policy Studies: A Practical Approach is an attempt to bring together the various aspects of educational policy "under one cover". Those aspects covered in Chapters 1-9 include what educational policy is all about, the values and principles inherent in educational policy, types of policies, policy analysis, policy development, implementation, evaluation and dissemination. Chapter 10 discusses the role research plays in the actual development of policy, and issues and concerns related to educational policy are the focus of Chapter 11. Chapter 12 examines the role of policy in educational reform, and what lies ahead in educational policy is the topic covered in Chapter 13.

There exists no shortage of books and writings on policy and educational policy which tend to focus on specific areas of policy study. Hopefully, this publication provides the reader with a holistic overview of educational policy while at the same time doing justice to the works of those writers who have contributed to the current literature on this topic. In many ways this handbook is a "discussion starter" in that it raises a number of points, concepts, issues and concerns which warrant additional follow-up. It will be of value to the reader looking for that "overview," whether that student be enrolled in a graduate course in education or a school board trustee seeking some practical information on educational policy.

CHAPTER 1
AN OVERVIEW OF EDUCATIONAL POLICY STUDIES

In recent years educational policy studies seem to have taken on a new significance. According to Boyd and Plank (1994) there appears to be a growing recognition of education as a strategic factor in national economic welfare and this has resulted in educational policy becoming a high priority issue. Silver (1995) goes so far to say that this latest concern with educational policy is indeed "policy rage" (p. 2). Whether these various perspectives are accurate or not, there is no doubt that in this latest wave of educational reform being experienced in North America, educational policy is being touted as a major concern especially in light of the various changes in educational governance both at the school building and school district levels.

What is Educational Policy Studies?

What do we mean when we employ the term "educational policy studies"? A number of "images" come to mind: research centered on the specific subject of the policy; decision-making, hopefully of the shared and collegial kind; the current state of what's happening with that particular subject – the positives and the negatives and various other related issues and concerns; and what the current research tells us with respect to that subject are but a few to keep in mind.

Nagel (1980) has suggested that policy studies are concerned with "the nature, causes, and effects of alternative public policies" (p. 391). A less erudite conceptualization of policy studies would be along the lines of policy analysis, policy development, policy implementation, policy evaluation and policy revision. Policy analysis would involve studying the issue and consulting with the key stakeholders to determine the "slant" which a specific policy should take. The other areas would involve the actual development and the related processes of implementing, evaluating and revising to ensure the policy achieves the objectives it was designed to achieve.

There is a certain degree of ambiguity associated with educational policy studies. According to Boyd and Plank (1994), "because of the richness and variety of purposes and approaches involved in policy studies, it is not surprising that there is ambiguity about what constitutes the field" (p. 1836). They attribute part of that difficulty as arising from the fact that the conception of the field has changed dramatically since its initial growth spurt in the early 1960s.

Wildavsky (1985) has concluded that the field has moved from a "macro-macho" approach to a "micro-incremental" approach:

> The origins of the 'macro-macho' versions of policy analysis
> – the belief that large national problems, from defense to
> welfare, are susceptible to solution through applications of
> economic analysis – were rooted in the intersection between
> economics, statistics, computing, and the defense 'think
> tanks' of the early 1960s. (p. 28)

It was assumed at the time that large-scale economic models could capture the complexity of policy problems and identify the most efficient policy alternatives; out of this tradition emerged an ambitious and robust paradigm for policy analysis that continues to influence the field today (Boyd & Plank, 1994).

In an effort to decrease that ambiguity, or as some critics might suggest, to perhaps add to that ambiguity, many graduate schools of education have now developed specific courses in educational policy studies. One would think that students pursuing graduate degrees in educational leadership and curriculum studies would be well served by having the opportunity to critically examine this whole area of educational policy. Educators, whether it be teachers in the classroom or the building or district level administrators, on a regular basis confront some aspect of policy in the multitude of decisions they make every day.

Policy Defined

There are as many definitions as there are writers on the subject. As Cunningham (1963) stated four decades ago, "policy is like an elephant – you recognize one when you see it, but it is somewhat more difficult to define" (p. 229) – a statement which is still relevant today. Duke and Canady (1991) have concluded that a commonly accepted definition of policy is still missing in both the literature and school practice. Definitions range from the very brief and to the point to ones which are rather long and convoluted. A sampling of these are presented here for your consideration.

Caldwell and Spinks (1988) define policy as "a statement of purpose and one or more broad guidelines as to how that purpose is to be achieved, which, taken together, provide a framework for the operation of the school or programme" (p. 41). They further state that policy may allow discretion in its implementation, with the basis for that discretion often stated as part of the policy.

Sergiovanni, Burlingame, Coombs, and Thurston (1999) refer to policy as "any authoritative communication about how individuals in certain positions should behave under specified conditions" (p. 230). They offer the following illustration:

> The principal who issues a memorandum saying that "no teacher should leave the building before 3:45 p.m. on school days" has fashioned a policy – so has the superintendent who directs principals not to suspend pupils for more than three days without board approval, and the state legislature that enacts a law requiring students to pass a competency test before high school graduation. (p. 230)

"A vision of where we want to go and guidelines for getting there" (p. 14) is how First (1992) characterizes policy. She goes on to say

> it is important that we agree that policy is wide, rather than narrow, long term rather than short term, and that it involves leadership. The leader is needed to paint that vision that becomes the policy statements. (p. 14)

Downey (1988) perceived policy as an instrument of governance and offered these two definitions:

> an authoritative determination, by a governing authority, of a society's intents and priorities and an authoritative allocation of resources to those intents and priorities; an authoritative guideline to institutions governed by the authority (and persons who work in them) as to what their intents are to be and how they are to set out to achieve them. (p. 10)

"A general approach to things, intended to guide behavior, and which has broad implications within a particular setting, whether it be a country, province or school" is how Levin and Young (1998, p. 60) describe policy. They go on to state that:

> policies shape the structure of schools, the resources available in schools, the curriculum, the teaching staff, and, to a considerable extent, the round of daily activities. Policies determine how much money is spent, by whom, and on what, how teachers are paid, how students are evaluated, and most other aspects of schools as we know them. The impact of policies can be illustrated by listing just a few areas of education policy. Some important policy areas [are] school consolidation, language policy, and Aboriginal education. (pp. 60-61)

Guba (1984, p. 65) has identified eight distinct concepts of policy, three of which are relevant here:

1. policy is an assertion of intents and goals;

2. policy is sanctioned behavior; and

3. policy is a norm of conduct characterized by consistency and regularity in some substantive action area.

Although the various writers and researchers of educational policy have their unique perspectives on what they consider policy to be, there are number of common elements inherent in their definitions:

1. that policy is a formalized act;

2. that policy has a pre-agreed objective;

3. that policy is approved or sanctioned by an institutional body or authority; and

4. that policy provides some kind of standard for measuring performance.

Benefits of Policy

The benefits of well-written, well-organized and continuously updated policies to any educational institution and its members should be obvious. Caldwell and Spinks (1988) provide the following list of such benefits:

1. Policies demonstrate that the school is being operated in an efficient and businesslike manner. When policies are written, there is rarely [any] ambiguity with regards to the goals of the school and how the school is to be administered.

2. Policies ensure to a considerable extent that there will be uniformity and consistency in decisions and in operational procedures. Good policy makes '*ad hoc*' or whimsical decision-making difficult.

3. Policies must be consistent with those for the system as a whole and with the various statutes which constitute school law. Policies thus add strength to the position of the head teacher and staff when possible legal actions arise.

4. Policies help ensure that meetings are orderly. Valuable time will be saved when a new problem can be handled quickly and effectively because of its relationship to an existing policy.

5. Policies foster stability and continuity: administrators and teachers may come and go but well-written and constantly updated policies remain. Such policies make clear the general 'direction' of the school, and therefore facilitate orientation of newly appointed members of staff of the school, and of the council or governing body, where such a group exists.

6. Policies provide the framework for planning in the school.

7. Policies assist the school in the assessment of the instructional program. Written and publicly disseminated statements of policy show that the policy group is willing to be held accountable for decisions.

8. Policies clarify functions and responsibilities of the policy group, head teacher and staff. All can work with greater efficiency, satisfaction and commitment when school policies are well known, understood and accepted. (p. 93)

Concluding Comment

This chapter has given an overview of what is meant by educational policy studies. Also discussed were a number of definitions of policy along with the benefits of policy. Chapter 2 looks at the various values and principles inherent in educational policy.

Discussion Questions

1. Should educational practitioners and theorists be concerned about educational policy studies? Why or why not?

2. What is your concept of educational policy studies?

3. Policy is sometimes referred to as the "foundation" of an organization. Is this true when we speak about educational organizations? Elaborate.

4. If you were designing a graduate course on educational policy studies, what would you consider as "key" components of such a course? Justify their inclusion in your course outline.

5. How would you define "educational policy"?

6. From your day-to-day work as an educator, what benefits of policy have you experienced?

CHAPTER 2
VALUES AND PRINCIPLES IN EDUCATIONAL POLICY

Developing educational policy with the concomitant processes is an exercise fraught with a multitude of values and principles. Taylor, Rizvi, Lingard and Henry (1997) speak about the competing interests in the policy process and the reality that policies represent compromises over struggles (p. 26). This competitive nature, they further suggest, highlights the "value laden nature of policies" (p. 27). Indeed, Prunty (1985) defines policy as "the authoritative allocation of values" (p. 136).

Values

In concurrence with this definition, it is quite obvious, according to Taylor et al. (1997), that power and control are two primary values in the policy-making process. As to whose interests these values represent, they proffer the following cogent perspective:

> First there are those accounts which accept a dispersal of values and power throughout society and argue that governments attempt to please as many interest groups in the policy process as possible. This is the *pluralist approach*. In contrast, the *elitist approach* sees governments as acting in relation to the values and interests of dominant groups. *Neo-marxist approaches* take this position even further in arguing that those who 'control' the economy have more political influence than others. Within such accounts there is a distinction between those who see this relationship as tightly deterministic and those who see it as more indirect — acknowledging that governments sometimes act against the interests of the economically powerful. *Feminist approaches* may be pluralist, elitist, or neo-marxist but all see the state as operating to reproduce male interests and power. (p. 27)

Pal (1987) has suggested that there are three types of values worth considering when dealing with public policy: content values; process values; and target group values. An examination of these values would seem to indicate a significant relevance to the study of educational policy. Consider the following:

1. Content values: Pal perceives these values as representing what should be done. In educational decision-making, which is at the very core of educational policy-making, there exists the age-old debate of centralization versus decentralization. Should decisions be made by a core group or should the decision-making process be open to a much wider involvement on the part of stakeholders. School-based management represents a movement which is designed to involve a grassroots participation in decision-making.

2. Process values: Pal considers these values as representing how to do something or, more specifically, how policies should be implemented and delivered. These are key questions that educators grapple with on a daily basis and which consume a considerable amount of valuable time, a commodity which is always in great demand in education.

3. Target group values: These, according to Pal, refer to "whom to do it for" (p. 209). The policy process by its very nature is full of competing interests and the various groups involved in those competing interests will obviously put forth claims that it is their specific group that is the more deserving. Pal speaks of two groups – those that are positively valued such as women, the elderly, the very young, the handicapped, small farmers, small business, and racial and religious minorities and those that are negatively valued such as large business, large unions and professionals. (p. 213)

These values cited above are significant for educators and deserve closer scrutiny when studying the policy-making process. Policy making is a complex process that is highly political as implied in the values discussed above.

A 1989 study by Mitchell, Wirt and Marshall (Wirt & Kirst, 1992) resulted in those researchers positing four values they consider to be "subsumed in school policy" (p. 82):

1.   Quality: This value is seen as "instrumental, a means to another value goal, namely the fulfillment of diverse human purposes, thereby making life worth living and individuals worthwhile."

2.   Efficiency: This value "takes two forms, economic (minimizing costs while maximizing gains) and accountability (oversight and control of the local exercise of power)."

3.   Equity: These researchers perceive equity as "the use of political authority to redistribute critical resources required for the satisfaction of human needs."

4.   Choice: This value refers to local school authorities having the opportunity to make policy decisions or to reject them. (p. 82)

According to Sergiovanni, Burlingame, Coombs and Thurston (1992),

> These are not the only values that enter into educational policy-making, but they are the four justifications for policies most frequently heard. Most of us prize each of these to some degree and, in fact, most policy issues involve more than one of them. Nevertheless, the position you take on issues will probably agree with your own sense of which values are most important. Which value you will defend most vigorously will depend on the role you play in the educational policy process as well as your own personal value hierarchy. (p. 223)

Pal (1992) emphasizes the ethical dimension of policy and suggests that in policy debates these ethical dimensions are either presented directly or are implied. He goes on to say that

> There are some policy areas where the ethical dimension appears muted, and others where it is the dominant chord. Economic policies, for example, are often discussed as though technical issues were paramount. Everyone appears to be in favor of economic growth; the question is how best, from a technical point of view, to stimulate that growth. Means cannot be divorced from ends, however, and each technical solution has consequences which may properly be judged on ethical grounds. Policy debates over discrimination, application of human rights legislation, education, cul-

ture, genetic engineering, abortion, and the family seem to hinge directly upon, or move very quickly to, issues of value such as freedom, individual rights, the proper role of the state, and the obligations and responsibilities of society to protect human life. In short, matters related to human sexuality, the sanctity of life, and traditional freedoms of speech and expression are self-evidently moral and ethical ones, and are forthrightly discussed in those terms. (p. 207)

Principles

In addition to the significance that values hold in educational policy studies, the subject of principles in educational policy is also a topic of major consideration. The distinction between values and principles is sometimes blurred in various educational issues but nonetheless, it is imperative that educators understand the differences when examining educational policy. The New Illustrated Webster's Dictionary (1992) defines value as something regarded as desirable, worthy or right as a belief, standard or precept (p. 1070). Principles, on the other hand, are defined as general truths or laws, basic to other truths (Webster, 1992, p. 770).

In educational policy studies, values are exactly as the name suggests – standards or precepts which the policy-maker considers so important as to have them permeate the specific policy. As discussed earlier, the value of choice is an excellent example. Principles are general truths which are kept in mind when developing various policies.

Gallagher (1992) considers principles as "decision criteria" which school boards and school administrators try to meet when developing and adopting new policies (p. 45).

She suggests four "decision criteria" or principles to keep in mind when discussing policy:

1. technical feasibility;

2. economic and financial possibility;

3. political viability;

4. administrative operability.

A brief overview of each of these follows.

Technical feasibility criteria measure whether policy or program outcomes achieve their purpose (Gallagher, 1992, p. 46). In other words, will this particular policy work in the real world and do what it is supposed to do? If it does, then it stands up to the test – it achieves or lives up to the principle of technical feasibility. She cautions however, that "when dealing with human behavior, no policy or program will always bring about its intended effect" (Gallagher, 1992, p. 46).

Economic and financial possibility measure two outcomes: the cost of policies or programs and the benefits of such policies and programs (Gallagher, 1992, p. 48). The key question here is whether or not the cost of developing and implementing the policy in question is justified in terms of the anticipated benefits and results. Unfortunately, one of the major criticisms of educational reform is that much of the reform initiatives are monetarily motivated and not driven by sound educational reasons. Policy is no exception to this thinking. There may be times in education when we have to "bite the bullet" and introduce policies that may be questionable from an economic perspective but extremely valid and desirable from an educational standpoint. After all, we are dealing with the lives and futures of our most precious resource – our children.

Political viability is another criterion or principle of considerable significance. Simply put, this refers to whether or not the policy will "fly" given the various stakeholders involved. Education is a highly politicized issue in today's society and if a policy is not acceptable to the relevant power groups, its successful implementation is in great jeopardy. Support for the policy must come from these groups or it is, in all probability, doomed to failure.

The final principle suggested by Gallagher (1992) is that of administrative operability. This refers to the practicality of the said policy. Are the financial and human resources available to implement the policy? Will teachers support the policy? Is the staffing available? Are the physical facilities available? These are but a few of the questions that need to be looked at under this umbrella of administrative operability.

Concluding Comment

When discussing values and principles on any subject in education, practitioners tend to become a tad impatient as it is sometimes a challenge to see where values and principles fit in the overall picture of educational policy making. This chapter has attempted to make that connection. It is imperative to see "the big picture" because values and principles are intricately intertwined in all aspects of educational policy. Chapter 3 examines the various types of educational policies.

Discussion Questions

1. Taylor et al. (1997) speak about the "value-laden nature of policies." Is this an appropriate descriptor of educational policies? Elaborate.

2. Are power and control inherent in the policy-making process? Explain.

3. Quality, efficiency, equity and choice permeate the literature on educational policy as key values. Choose a policy you have had some involvement in as an educator and discuss that policy in terms of these four key values.

4. Technical feasibility, economic and financial possibility, political viability and administrative operability are, according to Gallagher (1992), four important decision criteria to consider when discussing policy. Is this true for educational policy? Consider an educational policy you are aware of that was not successful in implementation; discuss that lack of success in terms of these four decision criteria.

CHAPTER 3
TYPES OF EDUCATIONAL POLICIES

According to Clemmer (1991), "there are many kinds of [educational] policies and they can be classified in many different ways, including purpose, subject, breadth of application, and derivation" (p. 164). He then goes on to categorize policies into four types: consequential, de facto, delegated and formal (p. 164). A brief explanation of each type follows.

Consequential Policies

Consequential policies are those "activated by several factors" (p. 164). These are policies which often result from outside forces or pressures such as provincial/state legislative actions. Clemmer sees these forces or pressures as imposing "controls and requirements that significantly affect the policies of local school districts" (p. 164).

De Facto Policies

De facto policies are "assumed from actions employees see about them which the viewers believe to constitute policy" (Clemmer, 1991, p. 164). These policies develop where no official or stated policy is written down and might be referred to as "unofficial policy" for lack of a better name. Over time these unofficial policies seem to become legitimated.

Delegated Policies

A third type of policy is categorized by Clemmer as delegated policies. These stem "from what is known in organizational circles as upward delegation" (p. 165). These policies result from situations where administrators do not know how a particular matter should be handled and so the responsibility for a decision is relegated "upstairs" to a superior. Delegated policies are fairly common as it is practically impossible to have a formal or official policy on everything that occurs in a school district on a daily basis.

Formal Policies

Formal policies are those which are consciously and officially developed by the educational organization whether it be the school district or the actual school. Clemmer (1991) describes this type of policy as going "through the formulation process of all formal policies, opportunity for public involvement, submission of administrative recommendations, and thorough review by all board members before adoption" (p. 166).

An Australian Classification

Another way of classifying policies is that of "...utilising binary distinctions" put forth by Australian policy researchers Taylor et al. (1997, p. 33). They further explain that "it is sometimes possible to classify an actual policy as manifesting characteristics of the two arms of the binary distinction within a category" (p. 33). Specifically, those distinctions are distributive and re-distributive, symbolic and material, rational and incremental, substantive and procedural, and regulatory and deregulatory.

Distributive vs. Re-distributive

Taylor et al. (1997) make the following distinctions between distributive and re-distributive:

> Distributive policies involve straightforward allocation of resources or benefits or entitlements, for example if an allowance is provided for all students for school books or uniforms. However, if such an allowance is provided to a target group through means testing, the policy could be said to be redistributive in character. Many special needs policies are of this redistributive nature, for example additional resources granted to schools under the Disadvantaged Schools Programme in Australia. Other redistributive policies would include special allowances made available for

geographically isolated students to attend boarding schools. (p. 33)

Symbolic vs. Material

The symbolic and material distinction

refers to the extent of commitment to implementation by those responsible for formulating a given policy. Material policies include a commitment to implementation through the provision of resources, whereas they are absent for symbolic policies. A good example of a symbolic policy is the Queensland Education Department's 1981 policy *Equality of Opportunity in Education for Girls and Boys* – just half a page in the *Education Gazette* (Lingard et al., 1987). This policy was developed in response both to the availability of Commonwealth funding and to pressures on the State department to develop such a policy. No state government funds were allocated and initially there was little attempt to implement the policy in schools. Symbolic policies tend to have broad, vague, ambiguous, abstract goal statements with little or no resource commitment and little thought given to implementation strategies. Indeed, the extent of resource commitment will often tell us much about the extent of political support for a given policy. In general then, symbolic policies are weaker than material policies. However, it should not be thought that symbolic policies are necessarily unimportant. Symbolic policies can have a strategic function in legitimizing the views of certain groups and altering the political climate in which issues are discussed. The development of a symbolic policy may be the first stage of an ongoing political strategy. Once an issue gets on to the policy agenda, pressure can be subsequently directed at strengthening the policy and the financial commitment to it – depending upon the extent of political support for the policy in the electorate. (Taylor et al., 1997, p. 34)

Rational vs. Incremental

Taylor et al. (1997) have this to say about rational and incremental approaches to policy:

rational advocates outline a set of prescriptive stages for the development of policy. On the other hand, incrementalists argue that policy development works over time by building on currently existing policies and practices. Even with a change of government, incrementalists argue that policy usually defines itself in relation to what went before. (p. 34)

Substantive vs. Procedural

Another distinction proffered by Taylor et al. (1997) is that of substantive and procedural:

Substantive policies deal with what governments are intending to do, and procedural policies with how things are to be done and by whom. For example, the Queensland Department of Education's Social Justice Strategy was developed in the early 1990s in the form of a brief rationale and statement of principles. As such, it could be said at that stage to have been a substantive policy. When it was fully developed with resources and guidelines for implementation, it could also be classified as a procedural policy because it outlined responsibilities for implementation across the system. (pp. 34-35)

Regulatory vs. Deregulatory

Regulatory and deregulatory are the final distinctions suggested by Taylor et al. (1997):

Policies in the equity and social justice area tend to be of a *regulatory* character, that is, they are about controlling practices. Thus, for example, sexual harassment policy seeks to prohibit certain behaviors. By contrast, *deregulatory* policies are usually associated with an ideological commitment to minimal government – or state intervention often associated with the release of market forces. Such policies are not concerned with overt control, though more subtle mechanisms of control may emerge in devolved systems. (p. 35)

Effect Category

Policies are very often categorized as to their effect. Clemmer's (1991) categories discuss policies in terms of what they want to accomplish. Specifically, those categories are: restrictive; nonrestrictive; prescriptive; and definitive policies. A brief description of each follows.

Restrictive

Restrictive policies are meant to narrow the operational choices of those who will implement them while allowing freedom to act within prescribed limits. Clemmer (1991) goes on to present some cautions when these kinds of policies are being considered.

> Such restrictions can be based on past experience or defensible apprehension but they should not reflect the special bias of one particularly conservative or liberal board member, nor should they imply that the board distrusts its administrators (even if it is true). When capable superintendents begin to feel unnecessarily hamstrung by policy restrictions, they become understandably restive. Restrictions on staff choices are not unreasonable (to allow total freedom is to invite anarchy), but whenever possible they should be reserved for administrative regulations and imposed sparingly at the policy level. (p. 171)

Nonrestrictive

Nonrestrictive policies are intended "to capitalize on the most professional and creative impulses of district employees at all levels" (Clemmer, 1991, p. 171). These are perceived in a very positive light:

> They perform an enabling function and allow for the broadest ranges of personal judgment. It is like telling the children they have full choice in what they watch but you expect them to show good judgment, adding that you do not expect the older ones to simply take over and impose inappropriate programs on their less powerful siblings, and that

each is at liberty to choose something else to do. In short, nonrestrictive policies express a board's implicit trust in the judgment of its administration. (p. 171)

Prescriptive

Prescriptive policies, according to Clemmer (1991), are utilized "where the board wishes to direct staff's actions, allowing virtually no deviations among schools or personnel" (p. 171). Again, Clemmer cautions against the use of such policies:

School district employees who view themselves as professionals – that's most of them in most districts – will tolerate the imposition of only a few prescriptive policies before becoming resentful. (In fact, the advent of collective bargaining in public education can probably be attributed more to unwarranted impositions on professional prerogatives than any other single factor.) Prescriptive policies reveal a patronizing attitude that – until adolescence – is more acceptable in a parent-child relationship than in one involving only adults who want to be viewed as co-contributors to a worthy enterprise. (p. 172)

McDonnell and Elmore Classification

One final method of categorizing types of policies is worthy of mention. Based on their research into the policy-making process, McDonnell and Elmore (1991) have developed four such types: mandates; inducements; capacity-building; and system-changing.

Mandates

Mandates refer to policies intended to produce compliance. According to McDonnell and Elmore (1991),

The benefits of mandates sometimes accrue primarily to specific individuals or groups, as for example, when handicapped or disadvantaged students benefit from federal or state-mandated programs in local schools. Often mandates are intended to benefit a broader community or society as a whole, as, for example, when polluters are required to install abatement equipment to reduce bad air or water. (pp. 164-165)

Inducements

McDonnell and Elmore (1991) define inducements as "transfers of money to individuals or agencies in return for the production of goods or services" (p. 165). They go on to state that

> because inducements are conditional grants for money, they are frequently accompanied by rules (often called regulations) designed to assure that money is used consistently with policy-makers' intent. The benefits of inducements accrue both to implementing agencies in the form of increased budget and authority, and to individual beneficiaries, through the value that is produced by the implementing agency. (p. 165)

Capacity-Building

A third policy type is that of capacity-building. Utilized when mandates and inducements are ineffective, investments in material, intellectual or human resources then become a policy option and are thus referred to as capacity-building (Clemmer, 1991). McDonnell and Elmore (1991) see the benefits of capacity-building accruing "in the short term to the specific individuals and the institutions that are their recipients, but the ultimate beneficiaries are future members of society, whose interests cannot be clearly determined in the present" (p. 166).

System-Changing

The final policy type articulated by McDonnell and Elmore (1991) is system-changing:

> the transfer of official authority among individuals and agencies. The expected effect of system-broadening or narrowing is a change in the institutional structure by which public goods and services are delivered and often a change

in the incentives which determine the nature and effects of those goods and services. (p. 166)

Concluding Comment

This chapter has discussed a variety of ways to categorize policies. Many similarities and differences characterize these categorizations. No matter what the category, it is incumbent upon the policy-maker and those students of policy making to carefully think through what the policy endeavors to accomplish. Educational policy analysis is the focus of Chapter 4.

Discussion Questions

1. Clemmer, McDonnell and Elmore, and Taylor et al. have put forth various categorizations for classifying policies. Compare and contrast any two of these classification systems.

2. What, if any, are the practical benefits of classifying policies? Elaborate.

3. In addition to those classifications discussed above, are there any other policy classification systems you could suggest?

CHAPTER 4
EDUCATIONAL POLICY ANALYSIS

There exists an abundance of definitions for educational policy analysis. This section will examine a number of definitions and then consider the various forms of analysis. A couple of practical models of analysis will also be presented for consideration.

Policy Analysis Defined

Downey (1988) in his work on educational policy referred to policy analysis as "the generation of information for the purpose of informing the policy-making process" (p. 12). He went on to suggest that this information gathering usually consisted of the following activities:

1. time-series, time-specific studies of trends and situation-specific studies, either of the school system itself or of its environment, for purposes of alerting school boards to the need for policy change;

2. the crafting of policy alternatives in response to the demonstrated need for policy change;

3. estimations of feasibility to help governing boards assess the consequences of adopting various policy alternatives. (pp. 12-13)

Taking a more holistic approach, Sandell (1977) in an earlier work on policy referred to policy analysis as "a set of procedures for inventing, anticipating, exploring, comparing, and articulating the alternatives available for achieving certain objectives. It is a method of managing... collecting and organizing... information. It is an effort to ease the consternation that stems from seeking better ways to ordain the process of decision making" (p. 48).

Gallagher (1992) proffers this explanation of what educational policy analysis is all about:

In its most general sense, *policy analysis* is the process of locating information relevant to the identified purpose. In this broad sense, *policy analysis* is synonymous with *problem solving*. Policy analysis has two characteristic features: the information collected has a practical orientation and the information will help guide action rather than be an end in itself. So the aim of policy analysis is to provide decision makers with information that can be used to make reasoned judgments in finding solutions to practical problems. (p. 4)

Pal (1987) takes a more erudite approach to defining policy analysis when he states that it is "the disciplined application of intellect to public problems" (p. 19). He further explains that:

1. the first feature of the definition is that policy analysis is a cognitive activity; it is about learning and thinking;

2. the second aspect of the definition is that policy analysis, as part of the collective policy process, is itself a collective activity;

3. the third feature of the definition is that it calls for the disciplined application of intellect meaning that policy problems have to be thought through if the activity is to count as analysis. (pp. 19-20)

In a more recent publication Pal (1997) quotes an explanation of policy analysis from one of his interviewees:

[Policy analysis is] a way of thinking, an ability to sift the extraneous from the essential, to get to the bottom, to see patterns and connections such as historical or international comparisons. It's the ability to think ahead a few moves, about the consequences downstream. It's the ability to organize information. (p. 15)

Taking a similar pragmatic view of policy analysis, Williams (1982) conceptualizes the term as "a means of synthesizing information including research results to produce a format for policy decisions (the laying out of alternative choices) and of determining future needs for policy-relevant information" (p. ix).

In that same vein, Quade (1975) writes "policy analysis searches for feasible courses of action, generating information and marshaling evidence of the benefits and other consequences that would follow their adoption and implementation, in order to help the policymaker choose the most advantageous action" (p. 5).

Policy analysis, according to Colebatch (1998), "commonly consists of techniques for identifying alternative courses of action, estimating their likely outcomes, and calculating which alternative best accomplishes known goals. These calculations yield 'objective' conclusions in support of one particular course of action" (p. 83). He further explains:

> This assumes that organizations exist to pursue goals, these goals are clear, and that the best way to pursue them is a technical matter which can be left to the experts. All of these assumptions are debatable. While it is assumed that organizations have goals, it is not always clear in practice what they are, how they have been chosen, or that organizational activity is best explained as an attempt to achieve these goals. And even if there are clear goals, it is not clear that participants are prepared to accept the judgement of an independent policy analyst about the best way to achieve them: policy inquiry appears to be about interaction and negotiation rather than about scientific detachment. (p. 83)

In his discussions on policy analysis, Ball (1994) suggests an open and creative approach which involves finding the appropriate theory and concepts for the specific task in question. He goes on to recommend the following: "The task, then, is to examine the moral order of reform and the relationship of reform to existing patterns of social inequality, bringing to bear those concepts and interpretive devices which offer the best possibilities of insight and understanding" (p. 2).

Taylor et al. (1997) offer this insight into what policy analysis is all about:

> In doing policy analysis, we need to keep in mind a distinction between policy *per se* and the substantive issues with which a specific policy deals. Some analysts suggest that the

very first task in policy analysis is to focus on the issue itself. There is a need to do this so we are able to assess how the policy is likely to work in relation to the problems it is addressing. For example, Gil suggests the first task in 'unravelling social policy' is 'to gain understanding of the issues that constitute the focus of a specific social policy which is being analyzed or developed. This involves explanation of the nature, scope, and distribution of these issues, and of causal theories concerning underlying dynamics' (1989:69). However, given that policy is often as much about problem setting as problem solving, there are often difficulties in separating the policy and the issues, because policies frame policy issues in particular ways. (pp. 39-40)

In his seminal work on policy analysis Wildavsky (1979) has this to say on our attempts to put forth a definitive definition of policy analysis:

there can be no one definition of policy analysis. As old-time cooks used to say when asked how much spice a recipe required, "as much as it takes". Policy analysis is an applied sub-field whose content cannot be determined by disciplinary boundaries but by whatever appears appropriate to the circumstances of the time and the nature of [the] problem. Do not ask from me what you should not want – a definitive definition of policy analysis good for all times, places, and circumstances. (p. 15)

Forms of Policy Analysis

As can be seen from the previous section, there is no one way of defining policy analysis. The same can be said when we examine the various forms of policy analysis.

Downey further elaborates on the insights he offered on the information-gathering activities associated with policy analysis (see earlier in this chapter under Policy Analysis Defined):

Stated differently, these information-gathering activities include: (1) the development of the accumulating data characteristic of traditional planning and management information systems; (2) the conduct of here-and-now evaluations of institutions or assessments of community needs; and (3) studies of the likely costs and benefits of specific policy changes. Analysis, then in its broadest sense, can be *descriptive* of ongoing trends, *appraisive* of existing conditions, and *anticipatory* of the consequences of possible policy changes. When analysis generates such information, it serves as the intelligence system for the policy making process. (p. 13)

Pal (1987) speaks about the three general styles of policy analysis: descriptive; process; and evaluation. He states that these three styles, "simply reflect orientations or intellectual postures toward policy questions" (p. 28). His description of each style follows.

Descriptive Analysis

[This style includes both content analysis and historical analysis.]

1. Content Analysis: In one sense content analysis is the most pedestrian type, but it is also one of the most important and frequently neglected. It is an empirical description of the content of an existing public policy, in terms of its intentions, problem definition, goals and instruments. This sort of description is frequently tedious and painstaking – if it is done well – but critical for most other types of analysis. One cannot assess the impact, logical consistency or ethical rationale of a policy unless one is absolutely clear about what that policy contains.

2. Historical Analysis: Any description of current policy requires at least a modest review of immediately preceding events. [This] goes well beyond, however, simply examining immediate antecedents. Instead, it assumes that current public policies can only be fully understood by examining their evolution, preferably from their inception in modern times. Whereas content analysis defines "policy" as what currently exists, the historical orientation tends to view policy more expansively, as a stable pattern of state behavior stretching over decades. Alternatively, if current policy is different from its earlier forms, a good way to understand it is to

examine these forms for contributions to and departures from current practice.

Process Analysis

[This] orientation pays less attention to content and its evolution and more to the process whereby that content is determined. Policy is seen as outcome, and while this orientation certainly tries to give a clear sketch of policy content, its main interest is in the causes of this content. It focuses on the immediate political process, decisions, debates, conflicts and compromises that produce public policy. This focus presumes that the political process and all of its complex interactions are responsible for the policy profile of a state at any given time. While recently there has been growing agreement in the academic literature that "politics matters," there is an argument that the pattern of public policy expenditures is best explained by broad environmental factors such as economic development, political culture, proportion of workers unionized, or exposure to international trade. A process focus suggests otherwise: policy is best explained with reference to the political system.

Evaluation Analysis

The third major style of policy analysis is evaluation. Rather than describing or explaining, evaluation aims in varying degrees at judging. It may judge logical consistency, efficiency or ethical character.

1. *Logical evaluation*: [This is similar to] content analysis in that it examines the current, detailed content of public policy. Rather than simply describing, however, logical analysis entails assessing a policy's internal rigor and consistency. Usually, this is not as complex as it sounds, at least when conducted by its major practitioners, media commentators and newspaper political columnists. It normally entails assessing a policy along one or a combination of the following dimensions: (i) internal consistency of the policy's multiple goals, (ii) consistency between goals and policy instruments, or ends and means, and (iii) the difference between intended and likely unintended consequences. The guiding

assumption behind all of these is that inconsistency is detrimental to intended policy outcomes. Policy "improvement" will occur to the degree that better consistency can be achieved.

2. *Empirical evaluation*: Public policies are problem-solving tools, so a major task of policy analysis is to see whether they work. Empirical evaluation encompasses a wide range of techniques to assess the efficiency and efficacy of a public policy. Insofar as logical policy evaluation also considers the likely consequences of policies, it includes a type of impact analysis. The distinguishing feature of the latter, however, is a concerted attempt to discover what the "real" effects are. Empirical inquiry replaces conjecture.

3. *Ethical evaluation*: Ethical evaluation assesses policies in terms of pre-existing value systems, of right and wrong. Many economic policies sometimes seem immune from this sort of analysis, hinging instead on questions of technical efficiency in reaching agreed goals such as lower inflation or increased investment. Other policy issues seem more obviously situated on an ethical terrain: prostitution, pornography, gay rights, school prayer, foreign aid to corrupt or cruel regimes, and abortion. The difference between these ethically-charged and technical policies, however, is more apparent than real. Efficiency, that shibboleth of apparently technical public policies, is entirely without ethical content, and so cannot be valued for its own sake. Concentration camps can be models of efficiency, but devoid of justice. On a more pedestrian level, an economic policy that encourages maximum labor productivity might countenance working conditions which undermine human dignity. (pp. 27-37)

A final comment by Pal (1987) on the various styles of policy analysis:

Good analysis is always grounded in solid description and historical understanding, though it may focus on logic, efficiency, efficacy, or ethics. As well, good policy analysis is usually comparative. Comparison does not constitute a style of its own, but is the deliberate selection of instances and counter-instances from other times and places. Comparison shows what is unique or routine about a given policy or policy proposal, and provides a broader canvas for assessment. (p. 37)

Policy Analysis Models

One such model for conducting policy analysis – CASA – is suggested by Gallagher (1992). The acronym CASA stands for Clear And Simple Analysis and is composed of five steps:

Step 1: Identifying the problem

Step 2: Defining policy decision criteria

Step 3: Developing policy alternatives

Step 4: Considering policy alternatives

Step 5: Presenting the policy choices. (pp. 6-12)

Identifying the Problem

At first blush this step would appear to be a relatively simple task. However, that might not necessarily be an accurate assessment of the complexities of the situation. Gallagher (1992) further clarifies:

> Because conditions change, the policy analyst must continually ask whether the problem that precipitated the search for a solution still exists. Often the analyst has to redefine the problem during analysis as it changes form or takes on new dimensions. In following the CASA model, the school policy analyst will analyze the best data available about the problem, settle on the criteria that will be used to evaluate alternative policies, think up possible alternatives, and then redefine the problem so that it can be reduced, controlled, and perhaps resolved with the information and resources on hand. Such an approach is often demanded by the immediacy of the problems found in public education and the short period during which the analysis must be conducted. (pp. 6-7)

Defining Policy Decision Criteria

A multitude of criteria exist for decision-makers to consider when developing new policies or revising old ones. These criteria could include financial considerations, legalities, political acceptability, efficiency, administrative ease or convenience, and efficiency (Gallagher, 1992).

Gallagher (1992) offers this sage advice to the policy analyst:

> Seldom are decision criteria of equal value to policymakers. The analyst will have to identify those criteria that are central to the problem under analysis and most relevant to the key participants in the decision process. Clarification of decision criteria early in the process helps to avoid the temptation to rationalize preferred options later. Similar to the ongoing nature of problem identification, new decision criteria may be unearthed during later steps of the analysis. (p. 9)

Developing Policy Alternatives

Having gone through steps one and two as described above, the policy analyst now has to develop a number of policy alternatives to be presented to the decision-makers. Gallagher (1992) cautions that "the challenge at this step in the CASA model is *to avoid prematurely limiting the number of policy options*" (p. 10).

How does the policy analyst go about developing these alternatives? Gallagher (1992) makes these suggestions:

> The analyst has several methods available: library research to find out what others have done, talking to experts (both other school officials and national consultants), and brainstorming. As values and assumptions of participants change over time, yesterday's unacceptable policy option may be today's consensus choice. (p. 10)

Considering Policy Alternatives

After a number of policy alternatives have been developed, the analyst then has to consider those alternatives in light of the identified problem and decision criteria. Gallagher (1992) has this to say with respect to that consideration:

> Careful consideration of alternatives will weed out realistic policy choices from pie-in-the-sky choices. Some alternatives may satisfy many decision criteria. Other alternatives can be discarded at this point because they violate the most salient decision criteria. Additional information may be needed to complete Step 4. At this step in CASA, the analyst may discover the problem has changed or that it no longer exists. This often can occur when the problem identification step resulted in inaccurate or incomplete analysis. This is not necessarily a negative development, however. It simply confirms the suggestion that, because the first attempt at problem identification is done quickly, several iterations through CASA will result in more relevant choices. (p. 11)

Presenting the Policy Choices

This fifth step in the CASA model is determined by "the relationship between the analyst and the policymaking body (the client)" (Gallagher, 1992, p. 11). The client may simply ask the analyst to present two to three viable options with the positives and negatives of each option. Or, the client may request all of the policy alternatives to be presented with the pros and cons of each and then make a decision based on that information.

Gallagher (1992) expounds on this process:

> In cases where the board of education is faced with competing political groups, and little consensus about anything exists, the analyst may lay out the options by displaying the political pros and cons. Use of political feasibility analysis can answer questions like these: What will the board have to give up or promise to have the policy alternative implemented? Will new administrative structures be required?

Does the board have the influence to implement a more comprehensive alternative as opposed to an alternative that solves part of the problem? Rarely is there one "best" alternative. Not only will different alternatives appeal to different political groups, but more than one alternative may solve the identified problem. Because making the policy choice is only part of the decision-making process, the policy analyst can help the decision makers consider the tasks and responsibilities involved in planning for the implementation and evaluation of the final choice. (p. 12)

Another policy analysis model worthy of consideration is the Realistic Model for Policy Analysis as developed by Brown (1996). Brown utilizes the image of the web to explain the intricacies of this model (p. 21): "At the centre of the web is a tangled core, the problem area (1). Radiating out from it, there is an intricate pattern of policy analysis, which requires clarification (2), decision-making (3), and finally problem formation (4). A brief discussion of each of these areas follows.

The Problem Area

With a preponderance of conflict involving values and goals in the policy-making process, Brown (1996) concludes that "it is little wonder that the problem area is messy, confused and poorly understood" (p. 22). She recommends that policy analysts, when first confronted with a problem area, need to try to clarify what it is all about.

Clarification

Brown perceives the clarification component as a "cognitive process that will require policy analysts to read, listen, interpret, learn, persuade, [and] reflect" (p. 23). Specifically, there will be a need to:

(a)   study existing policies and interests;

(b)   review available literature on the subject;

(c)   search for new information; and

(d)   establish parameters. (p. 23)

Decision-making

This third component is viewed as a process not a point event. According to Brown (1996), "policy analysts in education make most decisions under conditions that Collingridge (1980) refers to as Decisions Under Ignorance" (p. 25). She goes on to say that

> these decisions are interpreted, based on facts, values, and motivations, and are debated with other policy analysts/policy makers who hold conflicting interpretations. The clarification cycle referred to in the second component may be entered and re-entered many times, depending on the level and intensity of the debate. Tentative decisions will be made, but there will be a search to falsify, to look for and learn from errors. (p. 25)

Problem Formation

According to Brown, the end of the process of policy analysis is a tentative formulation of the problem, and the solutions. As she explains:

> In the final step, then, analysts provide the best interpretation that they can, of the problem, the solution. It is given cautiously, fully realizing that there will be an on-going search to falsify parts or all of it, that errors will be found, although it is as error-free as analysts can present it at this stage. It will ask for monitoring so that errors can be identified and modified as quickly as possible. (p. 26)

Tips for Good Policy Analysis

Pal (1992) offers us a number of valuable tips for good policy analysis with the caveat that such "tips will not necessarily guarantee good work but ignoring them is almost certain to lead to shoddy analysis" (p. 277):

1.   *Dive deep.* Good analysis is almost always distinguished by a solid historical grasp of the issues and the problem. In some cases, his-

torical depth may amount to no more than a few years; in others, it may require the analyst to retrieve decades of development and evolution. Background like this may never find its way into a report, and so it is tempting to skimp on it. The pressure of time also forces many analysts to do "quick and dirty" work. Avoid this, if possible.

2. *Know the law.* This maxim may lead the analyst through small mountains of legislative and judicial material, but it is the only way to crystallize the practical expression of policy. Analysis that confines itself to the rhetorical statements of intention that adorn policies inevitably will be misled.

3. *Count the stakes.* Every public policy is set against a political context of winners and losers, values and interests. Ignoring these is fatal, but a sensitive accounting is extremely difficult. Weighing those interests and judging their salience is also necessary. Finally, the analyst cannot simply reduce values to interests. In many cases, arguments of ethics or principles are merely smokescreens for self-interest, but in others, there are real values at stake which are unconnected to any obvious short-term interest. Good analysis tries to be sensitive to these distinctions, even if they cannot always be clearly made.

4. *Look at the big picture.* Practical policy analysis is usually undertaken at a specific level, e.g., should these subsidies be revised or this program changed? It is tempting to keep one's analytical nose down in the dirt without looking up at the bigger picture, the long-term trends. This occasional glance to the wider context is essential if analysis is to be imaginative, bold and fresh.

5. *Be cautiously skeptical of experts.* People usually become experts by concentrating on one thing for a long time. True experts do not merely know a field, they help shape and define it. Moreover, they may derive their livelihood from the field they study. As a consequence, they sometimes develop prejudices, perspectives, beliefs and convictions that blind them to new possibilities or different approaches. Good analysts use experts for help on detail and background, but are careful to solicit countervailing advice. If experts are to be consulted, always use more than one, preferably those known to have differing viewpoints.

6. *Be cautiously respectful of common sense.* The great conceit of modern science, social and natural, is its disdain for ordinary common sense. Policy analysis shares this conceit when it labels community preferences or common sense as "simplistic." People are never as stupid as they sometimes appear, and refined science can frequently paint itself into illogical corners.

7. *If possible, have a bias toward small solutions.* This is a variation of another, older maxim: "If it's not broken, don't fix it." "Improvement" for improvement's sake wastes time, money and energy; so too can over-ambitious, grandiose attacks on policy problems. In other words, "if it's broken, fix what's broken, and leave the rest." Small solutions are difficult to define, and this may seem like the road to conservative policy-making. However, the use of small increments to deal with problems is possible in most policy areas.

8. *Choose policy targets that you have a reasonable chance of controlling.* The global object of public policy is to change or maintain certain behaviors, but there is some wisdom in choosing means that can be reasonably well controlled and maintained. The point is not to abandon the more grandiose goals, but simply to reformulate them in terms more amenable to realistic policy intervention.

9. *Despite the above, remember that people have different preferences — try to structure choice into policy.* Policies that involve providing services to people should try to allow clients the maximum feasible autonomy. Individuals have different needs and interests, and no bureaucracy, however competent, can hope to second guess all of them.

10. *Be balanced in considering interests, but err on the side of widely-spread or diffuse interests over concentrated, organized interests.* Public policy is ultimately the expression of a community's sense of justice. It can no more be devoid of ethics than can any other part of the political process. (pp. 277-280)

Concluding Comment

This chapter has examined a variety of definitions of policy analysis and presented a couple of forms or styles of policy analysis. To bring this topic down to an operational level, two policy analysis models were put forth for consideration along with several tips on how to achieve good policy analysis. The next chapter looks at the actual development of policy.

Discussion Questions

1. Does "policy analysis" happen in the real world of education?

2. What factors might impede effective policy analysis?

3. How might some of these impediments be overcome?

4. Compare and contrast Gallagher's and Brown's models of policy analysis.

5. Does effective policy analysis ensure successful policy?

6. Pal's tips for good policy analysis speak to policy in general. How applicable are these tips to educational policy? Discuss using specific examples from your everyday work as an educator.

CHAPTER 5
POLICY DEVELOPMENT

Policy development refers to the actual formulation of policy. Policy development is "not a one-time activity" (Clemmer, 1991, p. 54) and is undertaken as a long-term process. Various authors suggest a rational approach to policy development which usually involves a set of chronological steps that include: problem identification, clarification of values, goals and objectives, and identification of options to achieve goals, cost/benefit analysis of options, selection of a course of action, evaluation of the course of action and modification to the program (Taylor et al., 1997, p. 25).

Elements of Policy Development

Carley (1980) suggests that there are three elements to policy development: making political decisions about which values will be allocated, then a rational determination through steps similar to those listed in the previous paragraph, and finally, the need to recognize that the bureaucratic structure will also impact upon the actual policy achieved.

Taylor et al. (1997) disagree with the rational notion of policy development and suggest that "in reality most policy is developed in a more disjointed, less rational and more political fashion" (p. 25). Their experience with policy making has lead them to believe that it is not possible to delineate and separate the elements so clearly:

> For example, one of us was involved in the development of a classification system for disadvantaged schools for a state department of education in Australia. We were required to utilise Australian Bureau of Statistics (ABS) data on a range of socio-economic measures to develop an index of disadvantage to classify schools so that equity monies could be distributed to those schools serving the most disadvantaged

communities. Supposedly, we were the 'rational' experts employed to carry out the technical work after the political decision to initiate the Disadvantaged Schools Program had been made. What we very quickly found, however, was that the seemingly rational process of creating indices of disadvantage was fraught with political questions of which statistics would be used – income, occupation, educational levels, housing, Aboriginality, and so on – to measure disadvantage. Further, one index meant that certain schools would receive benefits which would be denied to other schools, while different indices derived from different components from the ABS had different effects. In the end we accepted an index which most closely confirmed the 'expert' view of those who worked in the various regions of the State on the programme, indicating very clearly the ongoing and interactive rational/political character of the policy development process. (p. 26)

Approaches to Policy Development

Clemmer (1991) suggests four approaches to policy development:

1. starting from scratch;

2. revising and updating existing policies;

3. fashioning brand new policies; and

4. adding or changing administrative regulations.

In educational policy making all four approaches are fairly common but in recent years, with the advent of various reforms, it would seem that educators have been fairly preoccupied with revising and updating existing policies. This is particularly true with respect to reforms of a governance nature. A closer examination of each of these approaches follows.

Starting from scratch

This can be a lengthy and indeed onerous task. However, for practical purposes, it is suggested that a basic list of minimum essential policies be developed with a blueprint for the actual development of those policies. Such a blueprint would include: who would be the person(s) charged with ensuring the policy gets developed; what stakeholders should be involved; what role these stakeholders should play; what the timeline for development should be; and what kind of implementation is being recommended – widespread or pilot.

It is imperative that adequate time be allowed for public review and discussion of the draft policies. Stifling of these processes will almost automatically guarantee their failure from the beginning. Classroom teachers and building-level administrators can be highly critical of situations whereby they have not been given sufficient time for consultation and input. Considering that it is they who are the front-line implementers of most educational policies, such lack of foresight on the part of policy makers can quickly kill any policy initiative.

Revising and updating existing policies

Over time policies become outdated and a normal aspect of policy making is the revising and updating of existing policies. Clemmer (1991) offers this advice:

> In some cases it is harder to ferret out needed policy changes than it is to start from scratch. Most boards expect their superintendents and staff to constantly assess the effectiveness of current policies and regulations, and suggest needed policy changes or make desirable alterations in regulations. Though regular analysis of existing policies keeps revision at the level of "fine-tuning" and helps avoid the need for a major overhaul, new legislation or regulations at the national or state levels will often impose the need for drastic changes at the local level. (p. 57)

Fashioning brand new policies

Proactive leadership involves being on the "cutting edge" of policy formulation and educational leaders should always be on the alert for the need for new policies. Clemmer (1991) suggests that many policies are instituted because it is good practice to have them and that they let people know before anything happens how the board or the administration will normally act under a given set of circumstances (p. 58).

Adding or changing administrative regulations

Actual policies are primarily concerned with values and principles; regulations are the "nitty-gritty" which spell out the actual ways and means of achieving or living up to those values and principles. Because of this practicality, there will be times when such regulations necessitate revision. Conditions under which policies operate will vary from time to time and hence the need for such revision.

Senior administration should be cognizant of this need for revision and the onus is upon the administration to make such recommendations to the board. These recommendations will very often comprise the actual changes to the regulation(s) in question.

Policy Dissemination

Sometimes overlooked in policy development is the actual dissemination of the policy. After all, if there is not an effective procedure for getting information out on the new policy to those affected by it, then the process of policy development may have been for naught.

In the dissemination stage it is imperative that the policy maker anticipate and evaluate a variety of factors prior to deciding on the appropriate course of action. Such factors as the complexity of the policy changes, the degree to which the policy breaks with past tradition, the ability of personnel to put the policy into action successfully, and the possible conflict of the policy with vested interests are all considerations that need to be looked at very carefully when determining dissemination procedures. This topic will be discussed in greater detail in Chapter 8.

Policy Development Cycle

An actual policy development cycle as suggested by First (1992, pp. 229-231) may be helpful in our discussion of this topic. As First states, "policy development is continuous and overlapping. Various policies, problems, and domains will be in various steps of the cycle simultaneously" (p. 229). Each of these steps may have a variety of tasks which will vary depending upon the particular policy area being addressed. A summary of those fourteen steps follows.

Step 1. In Step 1 the need for attention to policy may happen in a variety of ways. This could range from a Supreme Court ruling to a school revising an existing policy.

Step 2. As a result of a particular issue, concern or problem being raised, existing policies are reviewed by staff to determine which ones need attention.

Step 3. Information necessary for consideration of the problem in question is gathered. This would involve research and literature reviews in addition to consultations with as many sources as possible – teachers, consultants, parents and the like.

Step 4. When sufficient information has been gathered, it is time for a committee to study, deliberate and determine the basic issues involved. This committee then fashions a report with recommendations for the board's consideration.

Step 5. The board receives the report and meaningful discussion ensues which will hopefully result in a consensus as to what direction the policy will eventually take.

Step 6. The work of writing the first draft of the policy in question is assigned to staff.

Step 7. Before the first reading and subsequent deliberations at a board meeting, the public and those most affected by the proposed policy must have adequate notice that the policy is being considered. Time for public commentary is then provided on the agenda of a future board meeting.

Step 8. Revisions and rewriting take place in response to the board's deliberations.

Step 9. At the next board meeting there is a second reading of the proposed policy and time is then provided for the public to have their input. The board may have further discussions as well.

Step 10. It is now time for final revision and for a careful review of the policy and its wording by legal counsel.

Step 11. At the time of the third reading at a board meeting, the board formally adopts the policy.

Step 12. The policy is then formally communicated to those immediately affected and the public at large.

Step 13. The policy is then implemented with plans for evaluation built into the implementation plan.

Step 14. The evaluation leads to revisions, updating and improvement and eventually to the starting over again of the policy development cycle.

Although the above steps appear to be very straightforward and at first glance perhaps simplistic and idealistic, one must realize that in the real world, the best-laid plans of mice and men don't always go the way we would like. Practicalities need to be kept in mind but the cycle does serve to give the student of policy a succinct and concise overview as to how such policy development is supposed to happen.

Concluding Comment

This chapter has given an overview of what is meant by policy development along with the various elements of and approaches to policy development. These approaches, together with the 14 step cycle, lean heavily on the practicality of policy development. Chapter 6 examines the concept of policy implementation.

Discussion Questions

1. Policy development is sometimes described as being reactive. Is this an accurate characterization?

2. Clemmer (1991) says that policy development is "not a one-time activity." Has your own personal experience(s), if any, with policy development given you any insight as to whether or not this is true?

3. How involved traditionally are teachers in the policy development process?

4. Do teachers perceive themselves as an intricate part of the policy development process?

5. How practical are Clemmer's approaches to policy development and First's 14 step policy development cycle?

CHAPTER 6
POLICY IMPLEMENTATION

Implementation Defined

Koenig (1986) writes that "The great Achilles heel of the policy process is implementation" (p. 149). Educators generally concede that the various other phases of policy making, such as policy analysis and policy development, are less challenging than actually implementing the policy in question. Implementation is where "the rubber hits the road" or as some educators would suggest, "where theory hits practice."

Often viewed as the link between policy production and policy practice, implementation of policy occurs in a highly complex social environment with official policy agendas seldom intersecting with local interests (Taylor et al., 1997).

A long-debated question about implementation is the degree to which it should be spelled out in the actual policy. Sergiovanni, Burlingame, Coombs and Thurston (1999) speak to this concern:

> Individuals charged with putting a policy into effect often complain about overprescriptive language that leaves them little room to tailor the implementation to local conditions. They would rather have policy-makers sketch out the grand design and leave the details to them. Policy-makers, on the other hand, recognizing how easy it is to subvert some policies at the implementation stage, may be blatantly prescriptive if they suspect that those charged with implementing the policy are less than enthusiastic about it. State legislators, for example, may want to leave very little discretion to local school boards or superintendents regarding how statewide high school graduation requirements are to be interpreted and implemented. (pp. 232-233)

Pal (1997) refers to implementation as the "execution" of the developed policy (p. 145). He further elaborates:

> Policy implementation is the stage of policy-making between the passage of a legislative act, the issuing of an executive order, the handing down of a judicial decision, or the promulgation of a regulatory rule, and the consequences of the policy for the people whom it affects. If the policy is inappropriate, if it cannot alleviate the problem for which it was designed, it will probably be a failure no matter how well it is implemented. (p. 146)

Approaches to Implementation

Colebatch (1998) suggests that there are two basic approaches to policy implementation – a vertical perspective and a horizontal perspective. He has this to say about the vertical perspective:

> In the vertical perspective, implementation means that authorized decisions at the top coincide exactly with outcomes at the bottom: it is a question of securing compliance. This is the (usually tacit) assumption on which much of the writing on the question is based: that the policy process is best understood as the formulation of goals by 'policy-makers', the selection of instruments to achieve them, and the assessment of the outcomes. This reflects constitutional models of government, and instrumental models of organization; it is seen as self-evident that those elected by the people to govern should be able to place their policies into action. (p. 65)

In making the comparison between the two approaches, Colebatch (1998) comments that

> In the horizontal dimension, implementation is an exercise in collective negotiation: the focus shifts from the desired outcome to the process and the people through which it would be accomplished. In the vertical dimension, the focus is on the policy goals, and people and organization come into the picture to the extent that they contribute (or

obstruct) these goals. The horizontal dimension recognizes that policy is an ongoing process, and that the participants have their own agenda and therefore their own distinct perspective on any policy issue. (p. 65)

Other examples frequently discussed in the policy studies literature are the top-down and bottom-up approaches articulated by Mazmanian and Sabatier, and Hjern respectively (Sabatier, 1993). According to Mazmanian and Sabatier, the essential features of a top-down approach are that it begins with a policy decision by governmental officials and then asks these questions:

1. To what extent were the actions of implementing officials and target groups consistent with (the objectives and procedures outlined in) that policy decision?

2. To what extent were the objectives attained over time, i.e. to what extent were the impacts consistent with the objectives?

3. What were the principal factors affecting policy outputs and impacts, both those relevant to the official as well as other politically significant ones?

4. How was the policy reformulated over time on the basis of experience? (p. 267)

The bottom-up approach, as explained by Hjern (1982), starts by identifying the network of actors involved in service delivery in one or more local areas and asks them about their goals, strategies, activities and contacts. It then utilizes the contacts as a vehicle for developing a network technique to identify the local, regional and national actors involved in the planning, financing and execution of the relevant governmental and non-governmental programs. This provides a mechanism for moving from street-level bureaucrats (the "bottom") up to the 'top' policy makers in both the public and private sectors.

In her review of the literature on policy implementation, LaRocque (1983) listed three such models: the classical or technological model, the political model, and the cultural or evolutionary model. Musella (1989) offers the following descriptions of these models:

1. Classical or technological model: [In this model] the relationship between policymakers and policy implementers is assumed to be hierarchical, that of super-ordinate to subordinate. Thus it is assumed that policy decisions at the super-ordinate level will be followed by implementation at the subordinate level. The role of the administrator is one of ensuring that policy change orders are carried out. If applied to all policies, then we can expect that board policy, along with administrative and supervisory direction, leads directly to the implementation of changes.

2. Political model: In the political model, the policy process is seen as a system of three environments, each with a specific function – policy formulation, policy implementation, policy evaluation. The relationship between policy makers and policy implementers is assumed to be based on a balance of power, with each group having different resources under its control. Hence, co-operation between implementers and policy makers must be negotiated.

3. Cultural or evolutionary model: In the cultural or evolutionary model, policy is assumed to be a set of multiple dispositions to act, the realization of which depends both on the intrinsic qualities of the policy and on the characteristics of the setting for implementation. In this model, the administrator and the supervisor must understand the environment and the "fit" of the specific change to the environment at the time in question. This model can be applied to most policy changes, if one assumes that the process leading to the policy change is just as important as the process that follows the policy change. (pp. 96-97)

Underlying Assumptions of Policy Implementation

Downey (1988) suggests that there are a number of assumptions to be kept in mind when implementing educational policy:

1. Educational institutions tend to be tradition-oriented and resistant to change; since policies are future-oriented and blueprints

for change, it is not surprising that they almost automatically generate negative reaction.

2.   Educational organizations are staffed by well-trained professionals; since policies tend to be shaped (or at least authorized) by lay boards, it is not surprising that they are almost automatically suspect.

3.   Though most governing authorities fully realize that the process of public policy development must unfold in the context of community power and politics, they frequently fail to realize that implementation must similarly unfold in the context of organizational power and politics. When the time for implementation arrives, internal politics and displays of power can thwart the process.

4.   The implementation of new policies almost always calls for new commitments and extra expenditures of effort; only under certain conditions can such new commitments and efforts be expected. (pp. 97-98)

Research Findings on Policy Implementation

Of all the aspects of policy, it is fair to say that policy implementation or rather successful policy implementation presents the greatest challenge to those working in the policy arena. It is therefore wise to consider what the research on policy implementation is telling us. In one such review of that literature on policy implementation research McLaughlin (1991) offers the following summary of "lessons":

1.   Perhaps the overarching, obvious conclusion running through empirical research on policy implementation is that it is incredibly hard to make something happen, most especially across layers of government and institutions. It's incredibly hard not just because social problems tend to be thorny. It's hard to make something happen primarily because policy-makers can't mandate what matters. We have learned that policy success depends critically on two broad factors: local capacity and will. Capacity, admittedly a difficult issue, is something that policy can address. Training can be offered. Dollars can be provided. Consultants

can be engaged to furnish missing expertise. But will, or the attitudes, motivation and beliefs that underline an implementer's response to a policy's goals or strategies, is less amenable to policy intervention.

2. Yet another lesson learned is that successful implementation generally requires a combination of pressure and support from policy (Elmore & McLaughlin, 1983; Fullan, 1986; McLaughlin & Pfeifer, 1988; Montjoy & O'Toole, 1979; Zald & Jacobs, 1978). Pressure by itself may be sufficient when policy implementation requires no additional resources or normative change. But pressure alone cannot effect those changes in attitudes, beliefs and routine practices typically assumed by reform policies. Opportunities for co-optation, symbolic response or non-compliance are multiple in the loosely structured, multi-layered world of schools and education policy, for example. Further, even an army of auditors would be unable to force compliance with the *spirit* of the law – which is what matters in the long run. District officials may be compelled to establish a parent involvement mechanism consistent with mandated practices, for example, but mandates cannot require them to welcome parents and facilitate their participation.

3. A related lesson from detailed studies of the implementation process is that change ultimately is a problem of the smallest unit. At each point in the policy process, a policy is transformed as individuals interpret and respond to it. What actually is delivered or provided under the aegis of a policy depends finally on the individual at the end of the line, or the "street level bureaucrat" (Weatherly & Lipsky, 1977).

4. We've [also] learned lessons about the importance of environment for both individuals and their institutions. Because implementation takes place in a fluid setting, implementation problems are never "solved." Rather they evolve through a multi-staged, iterative process. Every implementation action simultaneously changes policy problems, policy resources and policy objectives (Majone & Wildavsky, 1977). New issues, new requirements, new considerations emerge as the process unfolds. For example, the first challenges of implementation generally are to learn the rules of the game. What is supposed to be done? What

are the legal requirements determining program activities? Clear goals, well-specified statutes and effective authority are important *external* policy variables at this initial stage (Elmore & McLaughlin, 1983; Sabatier & Mazmanian, 1980). Generally, it is only after these compliance concerns have been understood that implementers can move on to address issues of program development or the *quality* of implementation. At this stage in the implementation process, external factors recede in importance as internal factors such as commitment, motivation and competence dominate.

5. We have learned that there are few "slam bang" policy effects. This is because policy effects necessarily are indirect, operating through and within the existing setting. Thus policy is transformed and adapted to conditions of the implementing unit. Consequently, local manifestation of state or federal policies will differ in fundamental respects and "effective implementation" may have different meanings in different settings. (pp. 187-190)

In summary, McLaughlin (1991) offers the following insights:

> Taken together, these lessons describe a model of implementation that moves from early notions of implementation as transmission or as a problem of incentives or authority to conceptions of implementation as bargaining and transformation (Ingram, 1977; Majone & Wildavsky, 1977; Ripley & Franklin, 1982, for example). This perspective on the implementation process highlights *individuals* rather than institutions and frames central implementation issues in terms of individual actor's incentives, beliefs, and capacity. Implementors at all levels of the system effectively negotiate their response, fitting their action to the multiple demands, priorities, and values of the policy itself. Further, this bargaining or negotiation is a continuous process, proceeding over time as policy resources, problems, and objectives evolve and are played against a dynamic institutional setting. This means that the nature of the bargain will change over time within settings and will most likely differ across units of the policy system. (p. 191)

Hogwood and Gunn (1993) drawing upon the work of a variety of policy researchers (Hood, 1976; Pressman & Wildavsky, 1973; Etzioni, 1976; Kaufman, 1971; Bardach, 1977; Van Meter & Van Horn, 1975; King, 1975) suggest that perfect policy implementation is virtually unattainable in practice. They go on to list a number of preconditions which would have to be satisfied if perfect implementation were to be achieved:

1. *The circumstances external to the implementing agency do not impose crippling constraints.* It is acknowledged that some obstacles to implementation are outside the control of administrators because they are external to the policy and the implementing agency. Some of these obstacles might be physical or political; there is very little, if anything, that administrators can do to overcome them except in their capacity as advisers, by ensuring that such possibilities are kept in mind during the policy-making stage.

2. *That adequate time and sufficient resources are made available to the program.* Policies that are physically or politically feasible may still fail to achieve stated intentions. A common reason is that too much is expected too soon, especially when attitudes or behavior are involved (as for example, in attempts to alter discriminatory attitudes towards the physically or mentally disabled). Another reason is that politicians sometimes will the policy "end" but not the "means," so that expenditure restrictions may starve a statutory program of adequate resources.

3. *That the required combination of resources is actually available.* This condition follows on from the second in that there must not only be constraints in terms of overall resources but also that, at each stage in the implementation process, the appropriate combination of resources must actually be available. In practice, there is often a 'bottleneck' which occurs when, say, a combination of money, manpower, land, equipment and building material has to come together to construct an emergency landing-strip for the RAF, but one or more of these is delayed and as a result the project as a whole is set back by several months.

4. *That the policy to be implemented is based upon a valid theory of cause and effect.* Policies are sometimes ineffective not because they are badly implemented, but because they are bad policies. That is, the policy may be based upon an inadequate understanding of a problem to be solved, its causes and cure, or of an opportunity, its nature, and what is needed to exploit it. Pressman and Wildavsky (1973) describe any policy as a 'hypothesis containing initial conditions and predicted consequences'. That is, the typical reasoning of the policy maker is along the lines of 'if X is done at time t(1) then Y will result at time t(2)'. Thus every policy incorporates a theory of cause and effect (normally unstated in practice) and, if the policy fails, it may be the underlying theory that is at fault rather than the execution of the policy.

5. *That the relationship between cause and effect is direct and that there are few, if any, intervening links.* Pressman and Wildavsky (1973) argue that policies which depend upon a long sequence of cause and effect relationships have a particular tendency to break down, since 'the longer the chain of causality, the more numerous the reciprocal relationships among the links and the more complex implementation becomes'. In other words, the more links in the chain, the greater the risk that some of them will prove to be poorly conceived or badly executed.

6. *That dependency relationships are minimal.* This condition of perfect implementation requires that there is a single implementing agency which need not depend on other agencies for success, or if other agencies must be involved, that the dependency relationships are minimal in number and importance. Where, as is often the case in practice, implementation requires not only a complex series of events and linkages but also agreement at each event among a large number of participants, then the probability of a successful or even a predictable outcome must be further reduced.

7. *That there is understanding of, and agreement on, objectives.* The requirement here is that there should be complete understanding of, and agreement on, the objectives to be achieved, and that these conditions should persist throughout the implementation process.

8. *That tasks are fully specified in correct sequence.* In moving towards agreed objectives it is possible to specify, in complete detail and perfect sequence, the tasks to be performed by each participant. The difficulties of achieving this condition of perfect implementation are obvious. Also, it is surely desirable as well as inevitable that there should be some room for discretion and improvisation in even the most carefully planned program.

9. *That there is perfect communication and co-ordination.* This precondition suggests that there must be perfect communication among and co-ordination of the various elements or agencies involved in the program. Even stating that perfect co-ordination is necessary, the reality is that such co-ordination is all but impossible. Communication has an important contribution to make to co-ordination and to implementation generally. However, perfect communication is as unattainable a condition as most of the others that have been discussed.

10. *That those in authority can demand and obtain perfect compliance.* The final and perhaps least attainable condition of perfect implementation is that those 'in authority' are also those 'in power' and that they are able to secure total and immediate compliance from others (both internal and external to the agency) whose consent and co-operation are required for the success of the program. The reality is that there may be conflicts between departments and agencies and those with the formal authority to demand co-operation may lack the power to back up those demands or the will to exercise it. (pp. 238-245)

Guidelines for Effective Implementation

Downey (1988) proffers the following guidelines which, although not guaranteeing perfect implementation, may facilitate varying degrees of successful or effective implementation:

1. The earlier staff members are involved in the policy-making process, the more likely they are to develop commitment to the policy and willingness to expand energy in its implementation.

2. The more precisely *patterns of participation* are planned and incorporated into the system's policies on policy making, the more effective involvement will be in its dual purpose of enhanc-

ing the policy-making capability and of developing commitment to enacted policies.

3.   The less a governing authority is required (or inclined) to flaunt its *powers of policy making*, the more likely it is to receive the co-operation of its staff.

4.   But, the less a governing authority and its executives are willing to *exercise authority*, when it is needed, the more likely they are to lose the respect of staff and the ability to exercise leadership.

5.   For a governing authority and its executives to assume that the participatory mode of policy-making requires less in the way of *co-ordination and facilitation* of staff effort, is to invite chaos in procedures and wastes of staff time and effort. (p. 101)

Concluding Comment

This chapter has emphasized the multitude of challenges to successful policy implementation. Specifically, what is meant by implementation was discussed along with a number of approaches or models of policy implementation. In an effort to prevent policy makers from "re-inventing the wheel," considerable attention was given to the various research findings on implementation. From those research findings emanate several strategies to assist the policy maker in what has been described as the "trickiest phase of policy." Chapter 7 looks at policy evaluation.

Discussion Questions

1.   Colebatch speaks about policy being implemented from either a vertical perspective or from a horizontal perspective. Mazmanian and Sabatier articulate the top-down approach and Hjern advocates a bottom-up approach. What approach or approaches have you personally experienced when policy or policies have been implemented?

2.   Various policy researchers have suggested that perfect implementation is unattainable. Do you think this is a valid assumption — why or why not?

3.   Do educators as a group want to be involved in the development of educational policy? Elaborate.

CHAPTER 7
POLICY EVALUATION

An obvious aspect of any form of policy development should be policy evaluation. Evaluation, as suggested by Downey (1988), is a process of determining the effectiveness and efficiency of policies in order to ascertain whether or not they have achieved their goals and intents. As Colebatch (1998) so succinctly states,

> evaluation completes the [policy-making] cycle; it enables policy-makers to know to what extent they are achieving their objectives, and to act accordingly. The common sense of evaluation is clear: if policy is concerned with achieving goals, then it is only sensible to check whether or not these have been attained. Managers want to be able to show that their programmes are effective. (p. 67)

Political Nature of Evaluation

While acknowledging the importance of evaluation, Pal (1997) comments on the highly political nature of the process:

> Consult any text on policy analysis and you will find passages extolling the indispensability of program evaluation. It could hardly be otherwise, given that program evaluation is primarily about trying to figure out how successful a policy has been, whether it met its objectives, how far it fell short, and what might be done to improve its impact. The same passages that extol evaluation, however, are usually complemented by ones that say that it is expensive, difficult, rarely conclusive, and politically unpopular. Precisely because evaluation is so potentially crucial to the fortunes of a policy or program, opponents and supporters work hard to get the evaluation results they need to strengthen their case. That is, if evaluation takes place at all. Not only is it politically sensitive (who wants to hear bad news?), it can seem secondary to the really important job of designing and implementing solutions to public problems. Policy evaluation therefore has

enjoyed more theoretical than practical popularity, and in Canada at least, has not been enthusiastically supported either as a government or a third party (i.e. foundations or think tanks) activity. This is changing. The new emphasis on results, coupled with a gradual shift to special operating agencies, contracted-out services, and partnerships, increases the need for evaluation because it puts new pressures on governments to be accountable. (p. 233)

Significance of Evaluation

Koenig (1986) emphasizes the significance of evaluation to the policy-making process:

> The availability of competently conducted and genuinely considered evaluation constitutes a critical juncture in democratic policy-making. Without a network of external evaluations, policy-making is not systematically reviewed and assessed but drones on in privacy, free to commit error and to expend resources profligately. Without competent evaluations, higher executives, legislatures and the citizenry will remain ignorant of the actual performance of policy-makers and implementers, and will lose their democratic birthright to judge, reward, and punish those who engage in policy acts, subject to their approval. (p. 183)

Evaluation of all policies should be an ongoing part of the policy development process, but as Clemmer (1991) suggests, "it is especially important with new policies or recent revisions, or in cases where enforcement is especially difficult" (p. 187). He goes on to make the following suggestion:

> One of the best evaluative questions asks members of the policy's "beneficiaries" if the policy is having its intended effect. Of course this presupposes a policy with a purpose, which ought to be a fair assumption. If, for example, the policy was designed to allow pupils more after-school help with classwork, the evaluator will want to know if children are in fact getting more help or if the help being received is in a form that is useful to the pupils. Do the regulations impose unnecessary restrictions in some schools that have

always provided extra help for pupils but not during the precise hours prescribed by the regulations? If so, perhaps the principal or the superintendent ought to allow more flexibility. (pp. 187-188)

Sergiovanni et al. (1999) suggest that very often policy evaluation calls for trained policy evaluators to come in and find out what the policy change has accomplished and how people feel about it. The reality, they go on to say, is that more often it will just be people somewhere in the school system saying, "This sure beats the way we used to do it!" or "I knew this wouldn't work!" (p. 233).

Criteria for Effective Policies

Keeping in mind this practicality that Sergiovanni alludes to, there are a number of criteria put forth by various authors that can be utilized in evaluating policy. One set of criteria suggested by Clemmer (1991) offers the following for our consideration:

1. *Pertinent.* Only policies on applicable topics deserve development time.

2. *Timely.* Policies should respond to actual needs but they should not be enacted until essential facts are known.

3. *Functional.* The policy should make possible that which needs to be done.

4. *Practicable.* If a policy cannot be implemented, do not adopt it. (pp. 104-105)

Clemmer follows up these criteria with this general commentary:

Although good policies allow for a reasonable measure of interpretation, they are stated in language specific enough that they provide real guidance. Good policies treat broad, general issues that have long-term implications; poor policies often respond to specific incidents and prescribe narrow judgments, and they often prove unenforceable. Unlike those fostered in a business, where profit is an abiding incentive, a school district's policies should enhance the achievement of its own goals, which are educational or service-oriented. Of course, if a policy is prescribed by a certain law, it should faithfully adhere to legislative intent, as interpreted by the state's attorney general or the courts. (p. 105)

Clemmer goes on to list several questions which could be used in the evaluation process:

1. Is the policy within the board's legal and moral areas of interest, authority and responsibility?

2. Does the policy express the district's values or intentions?

3. Is the policy statement general rather than specific?

4. Does the policy respond to a common set of circumstances?

5. Does the policy avoid making the board appear arbitrary or capricious?

6. Does the policy tell you who is affected by its implementation?

7. Does the policy tell you when it should be applied?

8. Does the policy conform to the normal appeal procedure?

9. Does the policy comply with existing policy or law?

10. Is the policy the result of local effort and not an "import"?

11. Does the policy reflect broad and deliberate discussion?

12. Can the policy's effectiveness be evaluated?

13. Is the policy educationally sound?

14. Exactly what is authorized or required by the policy? (p. 106)

Characteristics of Good Policies

According to Clemmer (1991), good policies allow for a reasonable measure of interpretation but at the same time, they are stated in language specific enough that they provide real guidance. One of the criticisms of policy over time is that depending on the wording, the policy can be somewhat restrictive. Clemmer's point is a valuable one because in education, where we deal on a daily basis with individuals and their complexities, there are very few issues of a black and white nature; rather things tend to be gray. It is incumbent upon those involved in developing educational policy to be cognizant of these complexities and to word policy in such a way as to allow for flexibility in dealing with the myriad issues educators face on a daily basis.

Another characteristic suggested by Clemmer is that for policies to be effective, they should remain consistent with other local policies. There may be older policies still on the books which will have to be removed to ensure this consistency. Current and up-to-date are also hallmarks of good policies according to Clemmer. Although this may, on first blush, appear to be common sense in nature, it bears mentioning here. And lastly, he suggests that sound [i.e. good] policies are proactive and reflect the personality of the organization they represent.

Types of Evaluation Studies

The following types of studies for evaluating policy are suggested by Koenig (1986): *policy outputs, policy impact or performance, goal achievement, program processes evaluation,* and *benefit-cost and cost effectiveness methodologies.* A description of each of these types follows:

1. *Policy outputs*: These encompass the tangible and symbolic manifestations of public policy, which are the observable indicators of what a government agency or program does. However while this information is useful, it tells little about the quality and the effects of the actual policy's performance and consequently may not be all that helpful in the evaluation process.

2. *Policy impact or performance*: These examine the extent to which a policy output has accomplished its assigned goals. It asks: has a policy or program caused a change in the intended direction? Impact evaluation focuses on the delineation of operationally

defined goals, the criteria of success and the measurement of progress toward goals. Implicit in impact evaluation are questions of causality: has a policy or program produced a change in the target population in the direction and to the degree that policymakers intended?

3. *Goal achievement:* This is a more intensive variant of impact evaluation: have the goals of a policy or program been achieved? Evaluation research employs objective, systematic methods to assess the extent the goals are realized and examines the factors underlying success and failure. This evaluative task becomes complicated, sometimes hopelessly so, when the political process by which goals are created leaves them in a murky state. Evaluating programs according to goal achievement becomes complex if some goals are attained more than others and if the goals are interrelated. A goal-achievement evaluation faces difficulties in fulfilling a common function of evaluations: enhancing the quality of future program activities. Many participants are involved in determining goals, allocating resources to achieve them, and in structuring and restructuring operations. If an evaluation illuminates ways to improve performance, securing their adoption becomes an enormous political task. Interest groups, congressional committees, and bureaucracies all have shared interests in preserving the status quo and its benefits of power and material gain. Greater efficiency, through adoption of changes illuminated by evaluation studies, becomes less desirable when compared to the already established largess, and even worse, by threatening its continuation. Not surprisingly, goal evaluations have not compiled good track records in leading to more effective programs. They are also bedeviled by an image of irrelevance in the eyes of those who, logically, should be most inclined to use them. Program managers who oversee the activities on which evaluations concentrate typically find evaluations largely unresponsive to their information needs, and they commonly dismiss them as too slow, too inconclusive and too prone to answer the wrong questions.

4. *Program processes evaluation:* This method centers on specific steps in an agency's work and performance, internal dynamics and actual operations to understand a program's strengths and

weaknesses. It examines why certain things are happening, how a program's parts fit together and how others (clients, legislators, higher executives) perceive the program. Emphasis is on how a product is produced rather than on the product itself. Process evaluation can light the way to better decision-making, improved procedures, more efficient funding and more productive program design.

5. *Benefit-cost and cost effectiveness methodologies*: These apply the test of efficiency in evaluating program expenditures. Costs and benefits are identified and measured, the balance between them is determined, and programs are judged according to their ability to generate more benefits than costs. This approach emphasizes measurable costs and benefits. It suffers the weakness of often ignoring non-quantifiable factors, the importance of which can render evaluation useless, if not dangerous. In social programs, which abound with non-quantifiable elements, the tendency is to over-stress their measurable features. Generally, program costs lend themselves more readily to quantification than program benefits. (pp. 191-193)

Concluding Comment

From what has been said on policy evaluation by the various experts, it is quite obvious that without such evaluation, policy remains impotent. Although there are a variety of evaluation techniques in vogue, the kind used is dependent on the particular sector and the intention of the specific policy.

This chapter has provided an overview of what evaluation entails with a particular emphasis on what constitutes good and effective policies. Various types of evaluation studies were also discussed. Chapter 8 considers the challenges presented in policy dissemination.

Discussion Questions

1. How significant to the policy-making process is policy evaluation?

2. From your experience as an educator involved with policy making, how political has policy evaluation been?

3. What questions would you engage in if you were tasked with the evaluation of a new policy on, for example, student supervision?

4. Who should be involved in policy evaluation and why?

5. Comment on your perceptions of the following stakeholders' roles in policy evaluation: teacher; school administrator; parent; school board trustee; school board superintendent.

CHAPTER 8
POLICY DISSEMINATION

Definition

Policy dissemination differs from implementation in that it refers to the process of making the various stakeholders aware of and informed about the policy in question. In fact, this is a vital aspect of the policy process because it is imperative that those intimately involved with its implementation know the various intricacies of the policy; otherwise, the policy is probably doomed to be ineffective. This is indeed a challenge in its own right and how the dissemination should happen needs to be given significant consideration.

Practical Level

Clemmer (1991) brings it down to a very practical level:

> Because relatively few persons may have assisted in the development of a particular policy, unless it is controversial and has attracted public attention the vast majority of... students, employees, and patrons will most likely be unaware of its existence or its implications. All major district players should be informed about the new policy and how it will be administered, but the audience of first magnitude is always the one comprised of the persons most *affected* by the policy.

> If K-12 music teachers are the beneficiaries (or "targets") of your new policy, you should probably make sure that every music teacher in the district receives a copy, along with a copy of the regulations. Other teacher groups, administrators, and classified personnel can receive theirs via the regular channels – usually the building's policy manual. (p. 186)

Scheirer and Griffith (1990) characterize dissemination as "the initial diffusion of information about the program [policy] among potential users" (p. 164). The quality of this information and how it is conveyed to potential users of the policy are very significant.

Acknowledging the "universal acceptance of dissemination" (p. 214) Knott and Wildavsky (1991) suggest that we should not take this universal acceptance at face value. In their words:

> the chorus of acclaim should be enough to warn us that the term may be vacuous, a convenient excuse for failures that may be attributed to the lack of this essential ingredient, whatever it is supposed to be. Are there no conditions under which dissemination might be counter-productive, the less done, the better? The interests of senders may not necessarily coincide with those of receivers. (p. 214)

Advice

When new policies are complex or involve new ways of behavior among institutional members, it may be necessary to lay the groundwork for such changes through conferences and discussions in addition to the more formal channels of communication (Rich, 1974). Rich goes on to offer this advice to the policy-maker:

> the policy-maker must anticipate and evaluate a host of factors prior to deciding on the proper course of action; such factors as the complexity of the policy changes, the degree to which the policy breaks with past practices, the ability of personnel to execute the policy successfully, and the possible conflict of the policy with vested interests are all matters that merit careful assessment in determining dissemination procedures. (p. 31)

Concluding Comment

This chapter has examined the difference between dissemination and implementation and has underscored the importance of dissemination. Although dissemination is closely linked to implementation, there are indeed differences but it needs to be said that successful dissemination is key to successful implementation. The policy-making process is such a complicated one that all too often, dissemination tends to be taken for granted. In the educational environment where time is an especially rare and precious commodity, this is particularly true of educational policy making. The onus is on those in leadership positions both at the building and district levels to ensure that dissemination is given the attention it warrants.

Chapter 9 examines the differences between policy and regulations.

Discussion Questions

1. Suggest a number of dissemination strategies which should facilitate the successful implementation of educational policy at the building level. At the district level.

2. In your experience as an educator, how much attention has been paid to policy dissemination? What problems with the dissemination process have you experienced?

3. How significant, in your opinion, is policy dissemination? Why?

CHAPTER 9
POLICY AND REGULATIONS

As mentioned earlier, policies serve as general guidelines. The specifics of the policy sometimes referred to as the "nuts and bolts" of the policy are covered in the regulations. Although there may be examples of policy which do not require regulations, more often than not, regulations are required to ensure the effective implementation of the policy. A number of writers on policy use the term "procedures" instead of regulations; in this publication both terms are used interchangeably.

Another way of looking at policy versus regulations is that policy refers to what needs to be done and regulations refer to how it gets done (Clemmer, 1991). Clemmer further clarifies this distinction:

> Whereas policies are designed as guides for discretionary action, regulations are formulated for the express purpose of delimiting the range of discretionary choices. Some regulations are stricter than others, but most include more verbs like must, shall, and will than do policies, in which may and should tend to be more prevalent. (p. 182)

Questions for Consideration

Clemmer (1991) has listed several questions that should be considered in the development of educational policy regulations or procedures:

1. Exactly what does the board want this policy to do?

2. What results will demonstrate that the policy is achieving the board's intent?

3. What does the policy require, permit or prohibit?

4. Are there laws or contracts that must be taken into account?

5. Will these regulations apply to the entire school system or only to one subdivision (e.g., school, class, grade)?

6. Would it be advisable to have the board approve these regulations?

7. Are these regulations too lenient or too strict?

8. What is the worst that can be said about these regulations?

9. What defense can be raised against these objections?

10. Am I willing to modify these regulations if they prove inappropriate? (p. 183)

It is quite obvious that these questions are rather basic and very practical, characteristics highly valuable to the policy-making process. Such characteristics will hopefully result in a set of regulations that are indeed realistic and workable.

Suggestions for the Writing of Regulations

Still relying on Clemmer (1991), the following suggestions are listed as guidelines for writers of effective regulations:

1. Keep the regulations as simple, concise and clear as possible. Avoid moralizing or preaching.

2. Be sure the target of the regulations is clearly spelled out. Determine who needs to care what the regulations say.

3. Be succinct and define important terms. Never assume that everyone will automatically know what you mean.

4. Use the present tense wherever possible. The future and the past are not a part of the here-and-now.

5. Do not be afraid to use imperative language (pupils will, teachers shall, principals must).

6. Say the most important things first. Start with the concrete and move to the abstract, as effective teachers do.

7. Use simple sentences. Complex sentences or requirements easily become confusing and counterproductive.

8. Note exceptions to one sentence in the very next sentence. People who need information fast do not read footnotes.

9. Check your regulations for clarity. Have someone not acquainted with the policy or the problem read each draft.

10. Be certain your regulations acknowledge the rights of all parties in the regulatory process. Foremost among these rights is the assurance of substantive due process.

11. If in doubt, have an attorney check the language of your regulations for legal implications. Good regulations should prevent litigation, not precipitate it. (pp. 184-185)

Policy Manual

One of the challenges of school administrators is keeping their heads above the continuous flow of paper that crosses their desks daily; keeping everything in order and easily accessible is not always an easy task. It is therefore recommended that a policy manual or handbook be developed to ensure that all policies with their attendant regulations and procedures are readily available. This manual is a "work in progress" and is never really completed as policies and regulations are continually being revised and updated. For reasons of practicality, a three-ring binder is therefore recommended as it allows for quick replacement of various pages.

The importance of the policy manual cannot be overstated. As First (1992) comments:

> the policy manual... should be a living document that serves as the chief guide for... management and, therefore, is a signpost for administrators, board members, teachers, and other staff who are responsible for carrying out their duties. Unfortunately, in today's legalistic world, policy manuals have become far thicker and wordier than they should be, but still they are very necessary and important enough that a district [or school] should make time and resources available to do a good job on the initial and subsequent updates. (p. 237)

Concluding Comment

Regulations/procedures play a very significant role in the policy process. This chapter has provided several practical suggestions for facilitating the actual writing of policy regulations. Not to be under-emphasized is the importance of the policy manual or handbook, which can be a real time-saver for busy administrators.

The role of research in the policy-making process is discussed in Chapter 10.

Discussion Questions

1. Policies versus regulations/procedures. Comment on your perceptions of these three terms.

2. Policies and regulations may be more commonly associated with school boards rather than school buildings. Is this an accurate perception? Why/why not?

3. What factor(s) may impede the formal development of regulations/procedures at the school building level? What suggestions would you put forth to help ameliorate this situation?

CHAPTER 10

THE ROLE OF RESEARCH IN POLICY MAKING

Significance of Research

What is the relationship between research and policy making? Does research have an influence on policy making? According to Berliner (1990), "research, unfortunately, either does not influence educational policy or influences it very slowly" (p. 263). He goes on to explain why this is so:

> First, policy in the educational arena influences large numbers of people who think that by virtue of having gone to school that they have informed opinions. Unlike, say, space policy, timber clearing policy, or rate setting policies for interstate commerce, educational policy is intertwined with the daily lives of people at the local level. More than in other areas of policy-making, educational policies often appear tied to the emotions, politics, social relationships, and fiscal interests of a local, vocal and broad-based constituency. When policy is made under such conditions, research ordinarily has a minor role to play. A second reason that research often fails to inform policy is that in many areas of intense public debate educational research has, until recently, been lacking or uninformative. (p. 263)

Clune (1993) has this to say about the importance of research to policy making:

> The importance of educational research is underestimated because much research is not useful, and much of the research that is useful shows that many educational practices are ineffective. But research findings about effective practices are gradually accumulating, and these tend to be quickly seized upon by a policy system that is hungry for solutions. Finding out how to increase educational achievement is a difficult task for everyone, including policy-makers and

practitioners; good research is needed to establish new directions. (p. 127)

In obvious disagreement with Clune's previous comments, Loveless (1998) elaborates on the perceived impotence of educational research:

> At its current stage of intellectual history, then, educational research is in a tenuous position, both in terms of its reputation as a disciplinary field within the academy and in terms of its standing as a body of verifiable knowledge. This state of affairs has important ramifications for the use of research findings in the real world. Research can offer only ambiguous direction to policy. The importance of this ambiguity is magnified because, with the traditional routes to academic prestige closed off, educational research must hunt elsewhere for legitimation. Policy-making forums are good places to look. The transaction that is offered to policy-makers is research for legitimacy. Researchers' reputations are enhanced when their ideas are realized in legislation or regulation. In return, policy-makers are able to claim that their initiatives reflect "what the research says" and they gain a stamp of scientific approval (even if quasi-scientific) for the causes they champion. These transactions are particularly powerful when it comes to educational reform since decision-makers routinely embrace findings that have not been tested or confirmed by practical application in classrooms. Compounding the error, when such findings are converted into substantive policy proposals, the ambiguities of research may be stripped away and forgotten. (pp. 282-283)

In a similar vein, Finn (1991) also takes a rather pessimistic view of how educational research has affected policy:

> To put it simply, our labors haven't produced enough findings that Americans can use or even see the use of. Over the past two decades, there has been a goodly amount of systematic inquiry and a flood of studies, reports, and recommendations, yet our education system has by many measures worsened. I do not say that research has caused the decline, only that it has failed to counteract it. Education

research has not fulfilled its role in the effort to improve our schools, perhaps because it runs into much skepticism from practitioners and policy-makers. Hence, its effects are limited, and this in turn fosters skepticism as to its potential – a wicked cycle. (p. 39)

Why Conduct Policy Research?

Ozga (2000) has advanced several arguments for policy research in education. She makes the point that education research should not be confined to the 'useful' or to research that improves pupil performance. Her contention is that "research should be useful, but usefulness is not a straightforward concept, and enhancing pupil performance, while desirable, is not a sufficient description of the proper and legitimate concerns of education research" (p. 5).

According to Ozga:

Teachers should engage in research, where possible and appropriate, in partnership with, and supported by higher education institutions. All teachers should be encouraged to feel themselves members of a research community, and should be enabled to participate in research debates, and to develop an orientation towards research and enquiry that carries into their professional practice. (p. 5)

Ozga (2000) further argues that policy research should be available as a resource and as an arena of activity for teachers in all sectors because of its capacity to inform their own policy directions and to encourage autonomous, critical judgement of government policy.

O'Reilly (1991) has this to say about the need for good educational policy research:

Fundamentally, we require good policy research to link the dominant national and provincial policies of state and governance to emerging changing views of the nature of learning, of education, of school, of organization, and of management. At the same time, we cannot allow corporatist, managerial policies, structures and relationships to be applied unthinkingly to education. Educational policies, structures and relationships must be embedded in the nature of education itself and in our beliefs of the nature of learning, of teaching and of child and youth development. (p. 5)

Cohen and Garet (1991) have concluded that "there is plenty of evidence that research affects policy, but generally this seems to happen in odd and unexpected ways" (p. 135). Specifically, they view most policy research, at least in education, as tending to have influenced the broad assumptions and beliefs underlying policies, not particular decisions. They go on to state that

Better methodology and policy relevance in applied research in education have not produced more convergent findings. This is in part because most policy-oriented research concerns programs with broad and conflicting aims, but it is also attributable to methodological conflict among research approaches and to the fact that the advance of applied research tends to complicate and redefine issues. As a result, improving applied research does not tend to produce more authoritative advice about social policy. (pp. 135-136)

On a More Optimistic Note

Suffice it to say that the relationship between research and policy is somewhat inconclusive. Berliner (1990), however, does express some optimism regarding that relationship:

The difficulty in setting and enforcing policy in education merely makes the task difficult, not impossible. As the research community in education grows and respect for the findings, concepts, theories, and technology that it yields also grows, we can expect more informed debates about educational policy. But the social, political, philosophical and fiscal issues that policy-makers must attend to always exert great influence on their decisions. Research must, therefore, be seen as just one of the many sources of information and beliefs from which policy is derived. We probably cannot improve much on our ranking in the set of concerns that policy-makers must consider. But we can improve on the quality and usefulness of our research, attempting in this way to illuminate some of the problems faced by those charged with the task of making educational policy. (p. 285)

Concluding Comment

Although the reviews on the relationship between research and policy are indeed mixed, one has to acknowledge that the potential for research impacting significantly on educational policy is considerable. Teachers are somewhat dubious about educational research and some of the reasons for this have already been alluded to in this chapter. One area of research not all that well known but with considerable potential is action research. In action research teachers function as researchers and collaborate with those in the academic community in efforts to solve real-life problems and challenges at the classroom level. It is incumbent on the academic community, especially those in faculties of education, to enter into partnerships with teachers to explore action research opportunities. Such initiatives may help bolster the reputation of educational research.

This chapter has examined the relationship between research and policy. Albeit, that relationship, depending on the perspective of the specific researcher, can be either positive or negative. Suffice it to say that there exists a tremendous potential for educational research to have a very significant impact on educational policy.

Chapter 11 examines a number of issues and concerns presently being raised in the educational policy arena.

Discussion Questions

1. Does research have a role to play in the development of educational policy? If so, what is that role?

2. What is your perception regarding the utility or lack of utility of educational research?

3. From your own experience as an educator, has research been utilized in policy development? If not, why not?

CHAPTER 11
ISSUES AND CONCERNS

In the preceding chapters of this handbook I have concentrated on the practicalities of educational policy. These practicalities have been gleaned from the writings of a variety of authors who have specialized not only in educational policy, but in policy in general. I will now examine a number of issues and concerns which have surfaced in the policy literature; some of those issues and concerns also emanate from my personal experience as a teacher and high school principal.

Those issues and concerns are as follows and are in no particular order of priority:

1. stakeholder involvement in the policy-making process;

2. the predominant model in the policy-making process;

3. the politics and ethics of policy making;

4. equity in educational policy; and

5. the link between policy and practice.

Stakeholder Involvement in the Policy-making Process

According to Clemmer (1991), "board, administration, staff, parents, students, and the community as a whole profit from the greater understanding and improved communication that an effective policy development process engenders" (p. 33). This comment assumes that there has been sufficient involvement by these various stakeholder groups in that process; such is not always the case. When this occurs, much disenchantment occurs and morale suffers.

Recently, there have been attempts in many jurisdictions to strengthen the role of local voices – particularly those of parents

– in the education system. This has been done by giving legal status to a variety of parent advisory committees, school councils and orientation committees at the school level, together with an elected membership and an expanded role in influencing the ongoing life of the school (Rideout, 1995). These initiatives have seen the inclusion of different "stakeholders" and have sought to include a greater advisory or consultative role for parents in a broad range of school-related issues (Levin & Young, 1998). One of the more obvious involvements by parents would be their input into the development of policies both at the building and district levels. My experience with this involvement has seen a greater reliance in recent years by the school board on such input and it is now quite common for school councils to be consulted on any new district initiative or policy. It is quite routine, of course, for the council to be involved in discussions related to initiatives and policies at the building level.

Concerns regarding the involvement of school councils centre around the amount of input parents actually have and the degree to which their input is considered at the district level. Special interest groups are always a concern and there are indeed times when one has to wonder whether or not parents are able to see the "big educational picture." Ideally, feedback from parents regarding district-wide issues through the school councils should ultimately reflect those "big picture" concerns; however, that is not always the case.

What is the role that teachers play in educational policy? Sergiovanni et al. (1999) comment that:

> Nowhere has the power structure of education changed more rapidly with respect to the role teachers play in the development of policy. For well over a century, teachers in this country [United States] have been organizing to further the cause of education and, in the process, to advance their own interests in the realm of school politics. In the last four decades, the movement has gathered steam rapidly. Some would argue that their organizations are destined to become

the dominant force in education policy, if they are not already. (p. 240)

Wirt and Kirst (1992) echo a similar sentiment:

No group has increased its influence on policy in recent decades as much as teachers. The timid rabbits of thirty years ago are today's ravaging tigers in the jungle of school systems. Unionism has produced this change, of course, and consequently made teachers a major political actor. (p. 207)

On a "macro-level," I have no argument with the above two statements. However, on a "micro-level" (i.e., district level), there appears to be some concern that teachers are not as involved as much as they perhaps should be. There also exists a perception that when they are involved in policy making, they do not have as much influence or impact on the actual policy developed. At the building level I acknowledge, from my own personal experience, that teachers do have a significant influence on school policies. This would seem to be rather obvious given the fact that teachers are "on the front lines" of education each day and in constant contact with the school administrators. The same is not necessarily the case when discussing policy development at the district level.

Another group which has traditionally not been involved in educational policies is students. In a number of jurisdictions where school councils have been set up, legislation calls for a student to sit on the council; this is usually applicable to high schools only. Levin and Young (1998) have this to say regarding student involvement in the policy-making process:

Since students are commonly cited by all parties as the prime beneficiaries of schools, and the reason we have schools, it seems odd that they have typically had no formal role in making decisions about various aspects of schooling. Considered from a political point of view, however, students have very little power. They lack organization, knowledge, wealth, and connections. As a result and despite the rhetoric, they can be – and often are – ignored when important decisions about their futures are being made. Where student involvement does exist, it is typically of a token nature, with little or no real influence on subsequent decisions. (p. 71)

The trend appears to be a more broadening of the composition of those stakeholders involved in the educational policy-making process. School councils also require a community member as part of their makeup. Various lobby groups are also consulted for their input as well. All indications are that gone are the days when policies were discussed and developed within the four walls of the schoolhouse or school district office. A major factor in this development is the role electronic media has played in reporting on the various educational issues; such reporting has heightened the awareness of parents and the community at large in matters of an educational nature.

The Pre-dominant Model in the Policy-making Process

Although school-based management is currently undergoing a renewed interest in educational circles, I would suggest that the policy-making process has been primarily a top-down affair whereby those in power have perceived a need for policy and have acted in such a manner to fulfill that need. Theoretically, there should be widespread involvement at the grassroots level. However, such is not always the case and because of the highly politicized nature of the policy-making process, certain groups dominate the process:

In the case of education, the policy process is often dominated by the established groups – governments and stakeholder organizations. They are already organized, and tend to have staff and money. The people know and are used to dealing with one another. They are already present in many of the decision-making forums. This fact tends to push the policy process in particular directions. Each group normally acts to protect the welfare of its own members. If the key decisions are being made by people who are already part of the system and benefiting from it, there might well be less likelihood of significant change. Those most in need of the political process to advance their interests – children, poor people, recent immigrants – are often least able to mobilize themselves to take advantage of it. Aboriginal people have often been excluded from political participation. So were women: being denied the vote, being unable to own property in their own name, and being economically dependent on men made it very difficult for women to establish a voice in educational governance. (Levin & Young, 1998, p. 73)

Although conceding that decision-making in education continues to be hierarchical, Owens (1998) does acknowledge a move more towards collaboration:

In traditional organizations [schools and school boards are prime examples], which are markedly hierarchical, the process of deciding how to make decisions is largely controlled by the administrator, not the followers. In such a case, the progress of the organization from autocratic decision making toward collaborative decision making resides largely in the extent to which the administrator sees power-sharing as a win-win proposition, a desirable state of affairs, rather than a threat to administrative hegemony. Many present-day educational organizations, though still hierarchical, have developed collaborative cultures to such an extent that reverting to the more primitive autocratic model would be difficult; the administrator is not so much confronted with the issue of whether or not others will be involved in the decision making but, rather, how and to what extent they will be involved. (p. 272)

Rational vs. Incremental

The policy-making process involves decision making and according to Hill (1997), "the controversy about the way policies should be made has been a dispute between an approach which is distinctly prescriptive – rational decision-making theory – and alternatives of a more pragmatic kind, which suggest that decision making is 'incrementalist', and that this offers the most effective way to reach accommodations between interests" (p.

99). The rational approach suggests that policy making is done in a logical, comprehensive and purposive manner (Simon, 1957).

Today we are aware of so many more complexities in the policy-making process that we are no longer sure of the right way or the wrong way; even to think of policy making in such terms would be an over-simplification. Lindblom (1959) has argued that policy making seldom proceeds in a very rational manner; he painted a picture of an organization which, instead of finding optimal solutions to problems, staggered uncertainly toward marginally better ways of handling them. Lindblom referred to this as the method of "successive approximations" (Braybrooke & Lindblom, 1970, pp. 123-124).

Sergiovanni et al. (1999) summarizes incrementalism as perceived by Lindblom and his followers:

> Gone was the notion of wise men sitting around solving recurring problems for all time. Replacing it was a notion of fallible human beings, limited in their abilities to see very far ahead, unable to examine all conceivable alternatives, set- tling for the first suggestion that promised to yield better results than the present policy. Lindblom and others who saw the same kind of limitations on rational policy making became known as incrementalists, and Lindblom (1959) dubbed his view the process of "muddling through" (pp. 79- 88).

From a practitioner's perspective, one would have to agree that policy making does not happen in a rational manner. Rather, as Lindblom and others have suggested, it is my opinion that "muddling through" is a very appropriate description of a process in education which in recent years has attempted to involve stakeholders at the grassroots level. However, it is rea- sonable to conclude that although there have been legitimate attempts to make that involvement happen, there still remains the challenge of actually having stakeholders meaningfully involved in that process.

The Politics and Ethics of Policy Making

One would like to think that all decisions and policies in education are taken and developed with the ultimate objective of what is in the best interests of students being the primary motivation. However, the reality is that this is not always so. Fullan (1991) refers to educational change as a "snarled process" and because educational policy is all about change, the phrase "snarled process" could also be utilized to describe the policy making process.

Thompson (1976) has defined politics as "the struggle over the allocation of social values and resources" which "involves making choices" (p. 3). Quoting Lasswell's definition of "who gets what, when and where," Thompson further suggests that "politics connotes the idea of people using influence and power to effect policies agreeable with their preferences" (p. 3). Both at the building and district levels, politics permeates the decision-making process. In an earlier chapter the importance of values in the policy making process was discussed and the political process is the medium by which those values are allocated. Educational policy making is all about values and the allocation of resources both financial and human, resources of which there are never enough to go around.

Politics involves individuals who often come together for purposes of solidarity and strength. In many jurisdictions in Canada, educational reform has involved reorganization of school systems and the resultant closure of school buildings with a whole list of related issues; this has forced individuals to band together in efforts to force the educational bureaucracies, whether they be school boards or ministries of education, to reverse various decisions. Hence, policy is developed in an environment where politics is rampant.

Enter the ethical perspectives on policy making. Ethics is all about doing the right thing for the right reason(s). One might conclude that this is a fairly straight-forward perspective but the waters become heavily muddied when politics is thrown in as another ingredient in the policy making process. Balance is the operative word and the onus is on those involved in the policy-making process to achieve such a balance, keeping in mind and considering the various political pressures and ethical concerns.

I am not convinced that this balance is always achieved and whether or not ethical concerns are commonly taken into consideration is indeed debatable at the best of times. The solution to this concern is not an easy one, but suffice it to say that the onus rests on those overseeing the policy process to ensure that such a balance is found.

Equity in Educational Policy

Equity is often defined in terms of equality of educational opportunity (Imber, 2001, p. 33). The concern here is whether or not educational policy addresses this notion of educational opportunity. Imber emphasizes the point thus:

> Every education policy maker and practitioner – from legislator and school board member to administrator and classroom teacher – is involved in the allocation of educational resources. While we often conceive of educational resources in terms of money (per-pupil expenditures), in reality they consist of a varied set of goods and services, and teacher time, attention and expertise. Together these goods and services make up the value of the education a student receives. (p. 33)

It is Imber's viewpoint that education policy and practice must be designed to promote the goal of creating the most equitable system of education possible (2001). He explains his perspective on equity in policy making:

> Equity should not be understood in terms of inputs, such as whether an equal amount of money is spent on each pupil because the same input can benefit some pupils much more than others. Nor should equity be understood in terms of outputs because achieving the same outputs with all pupils

is neither possible nor socially desirable. Rather, equity must be understood in terms of opportunity. All students have the right to benefit commensurate with the opportunity provided to other students. (p. 34)

Another way of looking at this whole notion of equity is in terms of fairness. A basic question that all policy makers need to ask themselves is whether or not the policy being contemplated is fair to those who will be most affected by it. A number of authors (e.g. Taylor, et al., 1997) discuss equity as social justice; this may be a more appropriate conceptualization.

A classic argument might have to do with a school district's per pupil grant to schools; the same kind of argument can also be made when discussing provincial/state grants to school districts. Should the grant to schools in an affluent part of the district be the same as that to schools in an economically depressed area where unemployment is rampant and achievement levels considerably below what they should be? In terms of fairness or social justice, one would probably respond that they should not be. Equality and equity are often used interchangeably; however, in the question just posed, an equal dollar amount does not mean that equity has been achieved. An earlier chapter examined the value-laden nature of policy making and nowhere is this more obvious than when discussing the provision of resources to educational organizations.

I suggest that this concept of equity be taken into consideration when educational policies are being developed and implemented. One must acknowledge the complexity of the policy-making process and that various aspects of that process, including development and implementation are never black and white. In the current climate of declining resources, financial and human, those charged with developing policies have difficult decisions to make; it is our best hope that this notion of equity in education be given the attention that it rightfully deserves.

The Link Between Policy and Practice

The recipients of many of the dicta resulting from educational policies are the teachers in the classroom. It is quite common to hear teachers comment that they are not interested in policy development as that is something that should be left to "administrative types" such as principals and school board officials. A major concern of teachers is the relevance of policy to what teachers actually do in the classroom – teaching. One reason for this perspective is that educational policy has traditionally been preoccupied with issues of a governance nature; pedagogy is very seldom addressed in educational policy.

Clune (1993) speaks to this concern:

Educational policy is typically fragmented and ineffective, producing a great volume of uncoordinated mandates, programs, and projects that provide no coherent direction, increase the complexity of educational governance and practice, and consume a lot of resources. The United States produces the largest quantity of educational policy in the world, and the least effective (pp. 126-127)

Bosetti (1991) calls for a more practical approach when he states that "more could be accomplished by the growing efforts to find the 'correct' policy solution in real life contexts. Academics can all too easily fall into the trap of trying to develop theory to explain reality, albeit imperfectly and then conduct critical analyses from the perspective that they should match theory" (p. 219).

Upon closer examination, it becomes self-evident just how important policies are to institutions such as schools and their practitioners. Keeping in mind that policies are the very foundation of the organization whether it be the school or the school district, it would be in teachers' best interests to pay more attention to this whole area of policy. Policy ultimately dictates what happens at the building and classroom levels and it is at these levels that teachers do their work on a daily basis.

Caldwell and Spinks (1988) acknowledge the difficulties associated with linking policies to programs:

> Policies are statements about substantive issues, including the curriculum, that contain the purposes to be achieved and the broad guidelines by which they can be achieved. Policy statements are prepared about such issues as mathematics, assessment of students, discipline, and reporting to parents. Programmes are natural divisions of the curriculum that reflect how the school is organised and how teachers work and children learn. Just as the set of policies will differ from school to school, so will the set of programmes. Some policies will link directly to programmes; for example, the policies on mathematics and physical education will be reflected in Mathematics and Physical Education Programmes, respectively, in most schools. However, this will not always be the case with all curriculum-related policies in all schools. (p. 115)

Concluding Comment

This chapter has focused on several issues and concerns related to educational policy. Perhaps the greatest challenge with respect to today's educational practitioner is for the practitioner to see the utility of the policy to everyday practice. The time devoted to policy development at the school level is woefully inadequate and this may account for the "disdain" that teachers often exhibit towards "policy." How to bridge that perceptual gap is a challenge to which there is no easy answer.

Chapter 12 considers the role of policy in educational reform.

Discussion Questions

1. Several issues and concerns have been listed in Chapter 11. List at least 2 other issues/concerns related to educational policy that you have personally experienced in everyday practice. Attempt to articulate solutions to these issues/concerns.

2. From your experience, is the top-down model of policy development and implementation changing to a more "grassroots" model? Elaborate.

CHAPTER 12
POLICY AND EDUCATIONAL REFORM

"Educational reform" seems to have been and perhaps continues to be the operative term in education in recent years. Educational reform is often discussed in terms of educational change; indeed, the two terms, from many perspectives, could be used interchangeably. What role does policy play in the reform/change process? This chapter examines that relationship.

The Relationship

That relationship is described by Taylor et al. (1997):

References to change have now become ubiquitous in politics and policy. At the same time few, if any, policies are entirely new; most are shaped by characteristics of previous policies. Policy is thus an instrument through which change is mapped onto existing policies, programmes or organisations, and onto the demands made by particular interest groups. To put forward a policy is to acknowledge that a new policy was needed or that the old policy needed to be revised in response to the changes occurring in society. (p. 5)

Challenges

Any educational reform or change process brings with it its share of challenges for those in the trenches. McLaughlin (1998) comments on those challenges:

teachers confront unprecedented demands for reform – calls for teachers to do better, and to do differently than they have done before. Efforts to raise standards for what students are expected to learn take place in the context of a "revolution" in cognitive science. New theories of learning frame new conceptions about important outcomes of learning and, by extension, ideas about school: higher-order thinking skills and deep understanding of the conceptual structures of knowledge domains take center stage in classroom instruction. Implied is a classroom environment more responsive to diverse student abilities and interests, where instruction emphasizes cooperative learning strategies, provides direct opportunities to construct knowledge and understanding, and incorporates performance assessments that tap students' conceptual development rather than mastery of rote knowledge. The extent to which teachers can succeed in meeting these goals depends on their success in wrestling with the deep, hard changes in beliefs, attitudes, and practices they assume. (p. 82)

Such expectations as listed by McLaughlin represent "mega-challenges" for today's teachers. Students come through our school doors carrying a multitude of "issues" with them – poverty and unemployment, physical and sexual abuse, inadequate parenting, family illness, one parent families, lack of nutrition and lack of sleep just to mention a few. This kind of baggage exacerbates the challenges teachers face every day and one can only ponder whether or not the reforms listed above are realistic and achievable.

Major Changes

These reforms would necessitate major changes in individual school operations and organization. Cohen and Spillane (1993) are less than optimistic as to the attainability of these changes:

One reason is that teachers and administrators would have a great deal to learn. It is unlikely they could offer the intellectually ambitious instruction that reformers seek unless they had ample time to learn on the job. Another reason is that the new instruction would be much more complex and demanding than the common fare in schools today. It is unlikely that teachers could do such work unless they had the autonomy to make complicated decisions, to work with colleagues, and to revise as they went. Still another reason is that teachers could hardly contribute to the development of a common instructional system unless they had much more time and opportunities to work with others in education beyond their school. How could these changes be made in the context of reforms that entail much greater central authority and power? This could not be done easily, unless the reforms were carefully designed to enhance such autonomy, and unless the capacities to exercise it were nurtured at all levels of education. (p. 81)

Similarly, O'Day and Smith (1993), when discussing this concept of reform, point out that the need for instructional reform is taken for granted in most policy circles. They comment further that:

> As official bodies endorse it [instructional reform] at national and state levels, as organizations of experts design national and state content frameworks and standards, and as curriculum and test developers redesign their materials to meet the new criteria, the concept of challenging content and higher-order skills takes on an aura of official policy. And with that aura of policy comes the responsibility of governments. Simple justice dictates that skills and knowledge deemed *necessary* for basic citizenship and economic opportunity be available to *all* future citizens – that is, access must be distributed equally, not just equitably. (p. 263)

One gets the impression that the call for educational reform has legitimated the forging of new policies. An obvious inherent danger is that the development of such policies can occur fairly quickly but the actual implementation with the requisite in-service work with stakeholders occurs at a much more "glacial pace." Taylor et al. (1997) have suggested that:

> the term 'reform' has become one of the most over-used ideas in the political vocabulary. It presupposes legitimacy and invites support for the ideas propagated in the particular policy. In this way, therefore, the state is not neutral with respect to the changes occurring in society, and its own interest in sponsoring some changes and preventing others is reflected in policy. (p. 5)

Characteristics

Darling-Hammond (1998) makes the point that "policy-makers who want teachers to succeed at new kinds of teaching must understand that the process of change requires time and opportunities for teachers to reconstruct their practice through intensive study and experimentation" (p. 654). She goes on to list four characteristics of policies necessary to achieve this:

1. Policies should first create extensive *learning opportunities* for teachers, administrators, parents, and community members, so that complex practices envisioned by ambitious learning goals have a chance to be studied, debated, tried out, analyzed, retried, and refined until they are well-understood and incorporated into the repertoire of those who teach and make decisions in schools.

2. Policies should allow for widespread *engagement* of a school's constituencies in the process of considering, developing, and enacting changes. For this to occur, communities must have a substantial role in constructing their own reforms rather than trying merely to implement ideas handed down to them by others – ideas which are bound to be poorly understood and mistrusted unless there is an opportunity to create adaptations that are valued and appropriate in the local context.

3. Policies should recognize the need for *simultaneous change* in all of the regularities of schooling that influence the possibilities for successful teaching of this kind. This means rethinking the array of policies – from school funding to teacher education to school accreditation to collective bargaining rules – that hold the current regularities of schooling so firmly in place.

4. Policies should be constructed in ways that maintain the *delicate balance* between external standards that press for improvement and the school autonomy needed to create an engine for internal change. (pp. 654-655)

Concluding Comment

Educational reform and related educational policies have not always been perceived as involving the front-line practitioners in education – teachers and building-level administrators. The current literature, as exemplified in the above commentary, seems to suggest that such involvement is a sine qua non; without such involvement reforms aimed at improving current classroom practice are doomed to failure. Educational policies have a significant role to play in the reform movement. They are the vehicle or medium by which changes and reforms can be initiated and legitimated. However, as suggested throughout this publication, practitioners need to be intimately involved in that development and implementation.

This chapter has examined the concept of educational reform and how educational policy fits into that concept. Chapter 13 looks at the future of educational policy.

Discussion Questions

1. What does the term "educational reform" mean to you?

2. What kinds of educational reforms have you personally experienced as an educator?

3. What do you perceive to be the relationship, if any, between policy and educational reform?

CHAPTER 13
THE FUTURE OF EDUCATIONAL POLICY

What lies ahead for educational policy? Will it take on greater prominence than it has in the past or will it continue to be relegated to the "back burners"? Not an easy question to answer, but it does deserve some pondering.

In Chapter 1 it was stated that our preoccupation with educational policy in recent years was characterized by Silver (1995) as "policy rage" (p. 2). I contend that this "policy rage" shows no sign of relenting; indeed I would suggest that it will be further amplified in the next several years. Why might this be so? Given the current pace of the reform/change process in education coupled with an ever-increasing emphasis on and perhaps even paranoia over liability concerns, policy will probably take on an even greater prominence in school and school district governance.

Over the past several decades we have traditionally looked to education for cures to all of our modern day social, economic and political problems. Schools have responded by taking on new non-educational roles – that of surrogate parent, social worker, policeman and pharmacist, to mention but a few. Policies have been developed in an attempt to clarify these new roles for educators. What has resulted are policy manuals large enough to act as door stoppers and which are very rarely consulted because of their sheer size and their legalese.

Coombs (1994) has suggested that if things continue to change so rapidly, "it is doubtful that much that we think we know about how education policy is formulated will be true 20 years from now" (p. 607). He elaborates:

> Tensions between the profession and the lay public will change in character as both the profession and the orientations of the public change. Relationships between the vari-

ous levels of educational policy making may change dramatically. It is difficult to identify laws, propositions, or even common knowledge that we confidently believe will survive these changes. (p. 607)

More Basic Research

The need for more basic research on education policy is identified by Coombs (1994) as a priority in the years ahead:

> Impatience with the limited payoff of basic research in education to date has prompted some to suggest that research efforts should be redirected toward applied research that would yield immediate dividends in the improvement of schools. There is, however, no certain way to improve educational outcomes without improving our knowledge of the policy process.

Policy Relevance

Policy relevance is suggested by Coombs (1994) as a major concern of the research that has been conducted. He recommends that more research is needed to probe the linkages between the preferences of constituents and the policy process as well as research examining the connection between educational policy and changes in educational outcomes. He goes on to state that:

> For basic research to be policy relevant, it is necessary to identify variables that are alterable through policy change and that will also bring about the kind of educational outcomes we seek. Until we have a much better idea of how interventions are likely to affect a student's academic achievement, conduct, attitudes (including educational aspirations), or access to continued schooling, for example, policy analysis is likely to continue to be a sometimes futile exercise. (p. 607)

Coombs (1994) has these suggestions with respect to the utilization of policy specialists outside the educational arena:

Attention to the demographic, social or economic changes that precipitate changes in education policy will require expertise from specialists in those areas. Closer examination of the impact of education policy on students will require methodological sophistication and intuition about schooling more likely to be found among educational researchers. Knowledge of the policy process alone leaves us far short of the capability to foresee changes in the environment that will stimulate new policy proposals, to predict the educational outcomes of proposed alternatives with confidence, and to make timely adjustments. Education policy analysis will have come of age when its theories and its methods are equal to that task. (p. 608)

Policy Coherence

Coupled with the call for greater policy relevance with respect to educational research is the concern being expressed regarding the lack of policy coherence. Cibulka (1999) has this to say about the lack of policy coherence:

the American system of public education is characterized by a lack of coherent policies extending from the federal level down to the local school, and extending laterally to other institutions such as employers. At the state level, for example, there seldom are policies that attempt to align policies pertaining to curriculum, student assessment, teacher certification and professional development, and finance. What is needed, in other words, is "systemic reform" so that policies and practices are more tightly coupled. In order for true reform to occur, it is necessary for these policies to penetrate to the 'core technology' of schools – "how teachers understand the nature of knowledge and the student(s) role in learning" and "how these ideas about knowledge and learning are manifested in teaching and classwork" (Elmore, 1996, pp. 294-295). Educational standards are the newest thrust in the systemic reform strategy. These standards serve as guides to the development of curricula and assessments. (p. 176)

Similarly, Fuhrman (1993) writes:

> A crisis of confidence surrounds education policy. Reformers despair at the failure of the "top-down reforms" of the early 1980s and of the unfulfilled promise of the "bottom-up", school-by-school change efforts of the later 1980s. The ability of the political system to deliver quality schooling is under attack. Many argue that policies should be abandoned altogether – by completely substituting market control or by removing policies so that schools can improve themselves unfettered. (p. 28)

However, all is not lost, as Fuhrman (1993) offers another approach for our consideration:

> However, the abandonment of policy does not offer hope of widespread improvement because schools cannot sustain self-generated change. Nor is school-by-school change likely to spread to all schools. The system must offer support. Systemic reform approaches suggest a way that the system can support school change, without either stifling school initiative or leaving schools to fare for themselves without help from the wider policy environment. Systemic reform approaches offer another possibility for those disappointed by policy, an approach to policy that combines centralized leadership around outcomes with decentralized decision making about practice. (p. 28)

Systemic Educational Policy

Congruent with Fuhrman's thinking above, Clune (1993) puts forth the concept of systemic educational policy, the idea behind which is "that the current policy goal of substantial increases in student achievement will require a major shift in a large number of educational policies" (p. 125).

The following five characteristics of systemic policy as suggested by Clune (1993) are worth considering:

1. Research-based goals for changes in educational practice and organization;

2. Working models of new practice and professionally accessible knowledge;

3. A centralized/decentralized change process;

4. Regular assessment of educational inputs, outcomes, and process;

5. A coherent, sustained, change-oriented political process. (pp. 127-130)

Although it is my contention that systemic educational policy is being developed to some degree at the present time, those efforts are at best "piecemeal" and much more needs to be done to bring about the desired results. With school improvement being the big picture goal of systemic educational policy, significant increases in student achievement represent a major part of that goal. If educational policy is to regain (i.e., if it ever had it in the first place) the stature and respect that it warrants, significant gains have to be made by the key players in the educational policy arena.

Concluding Comments

At the beginning of this chapter a couple of questions were posed:

1. What lies ahead for educational policy?

2. Will educational policy take on a greater prominence than it has in the past or will it be relegated to the "back burners"?

The foregoing commentary has attempted to consider those queries. Suffice it to say, that unless educators attach relevance and coherence to the policy-making process and the resultant policies, educational policy may go the way of the dodo bird.

Discussion Questions

1. Is there a future for educational policy? Elaborate.

2. What, in your opinion, needs to happen for educational policy to take on a greater importance in the lives of educational practitioners?

3. Centralized vs. decentralized decision making; where does educational policy making fit in? Elaborate.

CHAPTER 14
IN CONCLUSION

Summary

This publication has attempted to give a somewhat comprehensive and rather practical overview of the various aspects of educational policy studies. Those aspects include what is meant by educational policy studies along with the many facets of the policy making process: the values and principles inherent in educational policy; types of educational policy; policy analysis; policy development; policy implementation; policy evaluation; and policy dissemination. Also discussed were the topics of policy and regulations as well as a sampling of the various issues and concerns presently being experienced in educational policy. The role of policy in educational reform and the future of educational policy were also examined.

Although the approach to this topic of educational policy studies has been somewhat linear, I fully realize that in the real world of education – students, teachers, parents, administrators, school board personnel, board trustees and the day-to-day complexities of teaching and learning – educational policy is anything but linear. Linear evokes images of black and white and seldom any grey. Education policy, accompanied by a multitude of intricacies and complexities, is not like that. The linear approach does indeed suffice when one is writing a publication of this nature or when one is attempting to give a neat and tidy graduate lecture on the topic. However, it is imperative that the student of educational policy realize the variety of inherent complexities referred to earlier in this paragraph.

In order to appreciate the significance of these complexities, I consider the various "mechanics" of educational policy to also be of importance, but only to the degree that it allows the student of educational policy to come to the realization that educational policy is indeed complex. All facets of educational policy make up a process, albeit a "snarled process," a term coined by Fullan in describing the phenomenon of change in education but one which is also highly appropriate in characterizing the policy process.

Concluding Thoughts

What is the purpose of educational policy? Perhaps naively and a tad unrealistically, it is suggested here that educational policy should exist for the improvement of teaching and learning. In fact, Fuhrman (1993) goes so far as to state that "improving teaching and learning is at the heart of coherent education policy" (p. 320). Unfortunately, the educational waters get very muddied by such realities as the politics of education and a whole host of concomitant issues and concerns. And, ultimately, what is for the good of the student (i.e., the improvement of teaching and learning), as is so common and widespread in education, tends to get lost in the big picture and commonly falls through the cracks.

The Role of Teachers

McLaughlin (1987) has made the point that in education, it is the smallest unit, the classroom, that will ultimately determine the effectiveness of educational policy. Teachers operating in the classroom are at the centre of the teaching and learning situation. It is therefore of paramount importance that teachers understand "how policy can enable and facilitate" their work in the classroom (McLaughlin, 1991, p. 155). How this is done is indeed the challenge for policy makers. According to Taylor et al. (1997), educational policy does not deal directly with teaching and learning and "the implications of policies for these practices... are often left unstated and certainly under-theorised" (p. 173). Hence, teachers fail to see the value and the utility of many educational policies.

If greater attention were paid to teachers' interests in the policy-making process, then it stands to reason that teachers would be more involved with and pay more attention to educational policy. A pro-active approach, as opposed to a reactive one, would be to the advantage of teachers. That is indeed the challenge faced by teachers in an era where practitioners are expected to do more with less – less financial resources, less human resources.

The Role of School-Level Administrators

Although many of the comments made in the previous section are also applicable to the work that school administrators do, there are indeed areas where educational policies do impact directly on administrators. Granted, these have more to do with school governance issues and concerns; the challenge remains of connecting school governance with teaching and learning. This is a challenge that administrators should be capable of meeting and given the sheer volume of the literature on school reform, school improvement and educational change, the resources do exist and are very accessible.

Again, a pro-active approach is advocated on the part of administrators; easier said than done. Given the multitude of demands on administrators' daily agendas, no easy answer to these challenges is forthcoming.

A Guide and Facilitator

Suffice it to say that educational policy should serve to guide and facilitate our work as educators, whether we are teachers in the classroom, building administrators or school board officials. Educational policy in the big picture should serve to guide and facilitate teaching and learning. Unfortunately, as suggested previously, we very often get mired down in the politics of education and the student in the classroom suffers as a result. Policy can be restrictive and regressive if we allow it to be so. On the other hand, policy can guide us and facilitate the all-too-important work of teaching and learning. Policy then becomes the medium or vehicle by which we do that work – no more, no less.

REFERENCES

Ball, S.J. (1994). *Education reform: A critical and post-structural approach*. Buckingham, UK: Open University.

Bardach, E. (1977). *The implementation game*. Cambridge, MA: MIT Press.

Berliner, D. C. (1990). Research on teaching and educational policy. In L.R. Marcus & B.D. Stickney (Eds.), *Politics and policy in the age of education* (pp. 263-287). Springfield, IL: Charles C. Thomas.

Bosetti, R. (1991). The policy process in Alberta Education. In R.R. O'Reilly & C.J. Lautar (Eds.) *Policy research and development in Canadian education* (pp. 211-221). Calgary, AB: University of Calgary.

Boyd, W.L. & Plank, D.N. (1994). *The international encyclopedia of education* (2nd ed.). Pergamon.

Braybrooke, D. & Lindblom, C.E. (1970). *A strategy of decision: Policy evaluation as a social process*. New York: Free Press.

Brown, J. (1996). Policy and policymaking. L.B. Sheppard & J. Brown (Eds.), *Educational administration: Theory and practice* (pp. 1-30). St. John's, NF: Memorial University of Newfoundland.

Caldwell, B.J. & Spinks, J.M. (1988). *The self-managing school*. Philadelphia, PA: Falmer.

Carley, M. (1980). *Rational techniques in policy analysis*. Aldershot: Gower.

Cibulka, J.G. (1999). Ideological lenses for interpreting political and economic changes affecting schooling. In J. Murphy & K. Seashore Louis (Eds.), *Handbook of research on educational administration* (pp. 163-182). San Francisco: Jossey-Bass.

Clemmer, E.F. (1991). *The school policy handbook*. Needham Heights, MA: Allyn and Bacon.

Clune, W.H. (1993). Systemic educational policy: A conceptual framework. In S.H. Fuhrman (Ed.), *Designing coherent education policy: Improving the system* (pp. 125-140). San Francisco: Jossey-Bass.

Cohen, D.K. & Garet, M.S. (1991). Reforming education policy with applied social research. In D.S. Anderson & B.J. Biddle (Eds.), *Knowledge for policy: Improving education through research* (pp. 123-140). Bristol, PA: Falmer.

Cohen, D.K. & Spillane, J.P. (1993). Policy and practice: The relations between governance and instruction. In S.H. Fuhrman (Ed.), *Designing coherent education policy: Improving the system* (pp. 35-95). San Francisco: Jossey-Bass.

Colebatch, H.K. (1998). *Policy.* Minneapolis: University of Minnesota.

Collingridge, D. (1980). *The social control of technology.* New York: St. Martin's.

Coombs, F.S. (1994). Education policy. In S.S. Nagel (Ed.), *Encyclopedia of policy studies* (pp. 587-615). New York: Dekker.

Cunningham, G. (1963). Policy and practice. *Public Administration, 41,* 229-238.

Darling-Hammond, L. (1998). Policy and change: Getting beyond bureaucracy. In A. Hargreaves, A. Lieberman, M. Fullan & D. Hopkins (Eds.), *International handbook of educational change* (pp. 642-667). Dordrecht, The Netherlands: Kluwer.

Downey, L.W. (1988). *Policy analysis in education.* Calgary, AB: Detselig.

Duke, D.L. & Canady, R.L. (1991). *School policy.* New York: McGraw-Hill.

Elmore, R.F. (1996). Getting to scale with successful educational practices. In S.H. Fuhrman & J.A. O'Day (Eds.), *Rewards and reform: Creating incentives that work* (pp. 294-329). San Francisco: Jossey-Bass.

Elmore, R., & McLaughlin, M. (1983). The federal role in education: Learning from experience. *Education and Urban Society, 15*(3), 309-330.

Etzioni, A. (1976). *Social problems.* Englewood Cliffs, NJ: Prentice-Hall.

Finn, C.E. (1991). What ails education research? In D.S. Anderson & B.J. Biddle (Eds.), *Knowledge for policy: Improving education through research* (pp. 39-42). Bristol, PA: Falmer.

First, P.F. (1992). *Educational policy for school administrators.* Needham Heights, MA: Allyn and Bacon.

Fuhrman, S.H. (1993). The politics of coherence. In S.H. Fuhrman (Ed.), *Designing coherent education policy: Improving the system* (pp. 1-34). San Francisco: Jossey-Bass.

Fullan, M. (1986). "Performance appraisal and curriculum implementation research," Manuscript for the Conference on Performance Appraisal for Effective Schooling, Ontario Institute for Studies in Education, Toronto, February, 1986.

Gallagher, K.S. (1992). *Shaping school policy: Guide to choices, politics, and community relations.* Newbury Park, CA: Corwin.

Gil, D. (1989). *Unravelling social policy: Theory, analysis, and political action towards social inequality* (5th ed.). Rochester, VT: Schenkeman.

Guba, E.G. (1984). The effect of definition of "policy" on the nature and outcomes of policy analysis. *Educational Leadership, 42*(2), 63-70.

Hill, M. (1997). *The policy process in the modern state.* Hemel Hempstead, Hertfordshire: Prentice Hall.

Hjern, B. (1982). Implementation research – the link gone missing. *Journal of Public Policy, 2*(3), 301-308.

Hogwood, B. & Gunn, L. (1993). Why 'perfect implementation' is unattainable. In M. Hill (Ed.), *The policy process: A reader* (pp. 238-247). London: Harvester Wheatsheaf.

Hood, C.C. (1976). *The limits of administration.* London: Wiley.

Imber, M. (2001). The struggle for equity. *The American School Board Journal, 188*(8), 33-35.

Ingram, H. (1977). Policy implementation through bargaining: The case of federal grants-in-aid. *Public Policy, 25*(4), 499-526.

Kaufman, H. (1971). *The limits of organizational change.* Alabama: University of Alabama.

King, A. (1975). Overload: Problems of governing in the 1970s. *Political Studies, 23*, 284-296.

Knott, J. & Wildavsky, A. (1991). If dissemination is the solution, what is the problem? In D.S. Anderson & B.J. Biddle (Eds.), *Knowledge for policy: Improving education through research* (pp. 214-224). Bristol, PA: Falmer.

Koenig, L.W. (1986). *An introduction to public policy.* Englewood Cliffs, NJ: Prentice-Hall.

LaRocque, L. (1983). *Policy implementation in a school district.* Unpublished doctoral dissertation, Simon Fraser University, Vancouver, BC.

Levin, B. & Young, J. (1998). *Understanding Canadian schools: An introduction to educational administration.* Toronto, ON: Harcourt Brace.

Lindblom, C.E. (1959). The science of muddling through. *Public Administration Review, 19*, 79-88.

Lingard, B., Henry, M. & Taylor, S, (1987). A girl in a militant pose: A chronology of struggle in girls' education in Queensland. *British Journal of Sociology of Education, 8*(2), 136-152.

Loveless, T. (1998). The use and misuse of research in educational reform. In D. Ravitch (Ed.), *Brookings papers on education policy* (pp. 279-317). Washington, DC: The Brookings Institution.

Majone, G. & Wildavsky, A. (1977). Implementation as evolution. *Policy Studies Review Annual, 2*, 103-117.

McDonnell, L.M. & Elmore, R.F. (1991). Getting the job done: Alternative policy instruments. In A.R. Odden (Ed.), *Education policy implementation* (pp. 157-183). Albany, NY: State University of New York.

McLaughlin, M.W. (1987). Learning from experience: Lessons from policy implementation. *Educational Evaluation and Policy Analysis, 9*(2), 171-178.

McLaughlin, M.W. (1991). The Rand change agent study: Ten years later. In A.R. Odden (Ed.), *Education policy implementation* (pp. 143-155). Albany, NY: State University of New York.

McLaughlin, M.W. (1998). Listening and learning from the field: Tales of policy implementation and situated practice. In A. Hargreaves, A. Lieberman, M. Fullan & D. Hopkins (Eds.), *International handbook of educational change* (pp. 70-84). Dordrecht, The Netherlands: Kluwer.

McLaughlin, M.W. & Pfeifer, R.S. (1988). *Teacher evaluation: Learning for improvement and accountability.* New York: Teachers College Press.

Montjoy, R.S. & O'Toole, L.J. (1979). Toward a theory of policy implementation: An organizational perspective. *Public Administration Review,* September/October 1979, 465-476.

Musella, D.F. (1989). Problems in policy implementation. In M. Holmes, K.A. Leithwood & D.F. Musella (Eds.), *Educational policy for effective schools* (pp. 96-97). Toronto: OISE.

Nagel, S.S. (1980). The policy studies perspective. *Public Administration Review, 40,* 391-396.

New illustrated Webster's dictionary (1992). New York: PAMCO

O'Day, J.A. & Smith, M.S. (1993). Systemic reform and educational opportunity. In S.H. Fuhrman (Ed.), *Designing coherent educational policy: Improving the system* (pp. 250-312). San Francisco: Jossey-Bass.

O'Reilly, R.R. (1991). Educational policy research in Canada. In R.R. O'Reilly & C.J. Lautar (Eds.), *Policy research and development in Canadian education* (pp. 1-5). Calgary, AB: University of Calgary.

Owens, R.G. (1998). *Organizational behavior in education.* Needham Heights, MA: Allyn and Bacon.

Ozga, J. (2000). *Policy research in educational settings.* Philadelphia, PA: Open University.

Pal, L.A. (1987). *Public policy analysis: An introduction.* Toronto, ON: Methuen.

Pal, L.A. (1992). *Public policy analysis: An introduction* (2nd ed.). Scarborough, ON: Nelson Canada.

Pal, L.A. (1997). *Beyond policy analysis: Public issue management in turbulent times.* Scarborough, ON: ITP Nelson.

Pressman, J.I. & Wildavsky, A. (1973). *Implementation.* Berkeley: University of California.

Prunty, J. (1985). Signposts for a critical educational policy analysis. *Australian Journal of Education, 29*(2), 133-140.

Quade, E.S. (1975). *Analysis for public decisions.* New York: American Elsevier.

Rich, J.M. (1974). *New directions in educational policy.* Lincoln, NE: Professional Educators.

Rideout, D. (1995). School councils in Canada: A cross-country survey. *Education Canada, 35*(2), 12-18.

Ripley, R.B. & Franklin, G.A. (1982). *Bureaucracy and policy implementation.* Homewood, IL: Dorsey.

Sabatier, P. (1993). Top-down and bottom-up approaches to implementation research. In M. Hill (Ed.), *The policy process: A reader* (pp. 266-293). Hemel Hempstead, Hertfordshire: Harvester Wheatsheaf.

Sabatier, P., & Mazmanian, D. (1980). The implementation of public policy: A framework of analysis. *Policy Studies Journal, 8*(4), 538-560.

Sandell, S. (1977). Does your board need its own policy analyst? *The American School Board Journal, 10*, 48-49.

Scheirer, M.A. & Griffith, J. (1990). Studying micro-implementation empirically: Lessons and dilemmas. In D.J. Palumbo & D.J. Calista (Eds.), *Implementation and the policy process: Opening up the black box* (pp. 163-179). Westport, CT: Greenwood.

Sergiovanni, T.J., Burlingame, M., Coombs, F.S. & Thurston, P.W. (1992). *Educational governance and administration* (3rd ed.). Needham Heights, MA: Allyn & Bacon.

Sergiovanni, T.J., Burlingame, M., Coombs, F.S. & Thurston, P.W. (1999). *Educational governance and administration* (4th ed.). Needham Heights, MA: Allyn & Bacon.

Silver, H. (1995). Policy problems in time. In E.W. Ricker & B.A. Wood (Eds.), *Historical perspectives on educational policy in Canada: Issues, debates and case studies* (pp. 30-40). Toronto: Canadian Scholars' Press.

Simon, H.A. (1957). *Administrative behavior*. New York: Macmillan.

Taylor, S., Rizvi, F., Lingard, B. & Henry, M. (1997). *Educational policy and the politics of change*. London: Routledge.

Thompson, J.T. (1976). *Policymaking in American public education*. Englewood Cliffs, NJ: Prentice Hall.

Van Meter, D. & Van Horn, C.E. (1975). The policy implementation process: A conceptual framework. *Administration and Society, 6*(4), 445-488.

Weatherly, R. & Lipsky, M. (1977). Street-level bureaucrats and institutional innovation: Implementing special education reform. *Harvard Educational Review, 47*(2), 171-197.

Wildavsky, A. (1979). *Speaking truth to power: The art and craft of policy analysis*. Boston: Little, Brown and Company.

Wildavsky, A. (1985). The once and future school of public policy. *Public Interest, 79* (Spring), 25-41.

Williams, W. (1982). *Studying implementation: Methodological and administrative issues*. Chatham, NJ: Chatham House.

Wirt, F.M. & Kirst, M.W. (1992). *Schools in conflict*. Berkeley, CA: McCutchan.

Zald, M.N. & Jacobs, J. (1978). Compliance/incentive classifications of organizations: Underlying dimensions. *Administration and Society, 9*(4), 403-424.

Index